# Analytical Thinking for **ADVANCED LEARNERS**

Grades 3–5

*Analytical Thinking for Advanced Learners, Grades 3–5* will teach students to think scientifically, systematically, and logically about questions and problems.

Thinking analytically is a skill which helps students break down complex ideas into smaller parts in order to develop hypotheses and eventually reach a solution. Working through the lessons and handouts in this book, students will learn strategies and specific academic vocabulary in the sub-skills of noticing details, asking questions, classifying and organizing information, making hypotheses, conducting experiments, interpreting data, and drawing conclusions. The curriculum provides cohesive, scaffolded lessons to teach each targeted area of competency, followed by authentic application activities for students to then apply their newly developed skill set.

This book can be used as a stand-alone gifted curriculum or as part of an integrated curriculum. Each lesson ties in both reading and metacognitive skills, making it easy for teachers to incorporate into a variety of contexts.

**Emily Hollett** and **Anna Cassalia** are award-winning gifted educators and instructional differentiation coaches with Williamson County Schools, Tennessee.

Discover the other books in the Integrated Lessons in Higher Order Thinking Skills series

Available from Routledge
(www.routledge.com)

**Convergent Thinking for Advanced Learners, Grades 3–5**
Emily Hollett and Anna Cassalia

**Divergent Thinking for Advanced Learners, Grades 3–5**
Emily Hollett and Anna Cassalia

**Evaluative Thinking for Advanced Learners, Grades 3–5**
Emily Hollett and Anna Cassalia

**Visual-Spatial Thinking for Advanced Learners, Grades 3–5**
Emily Hollett and Anna Cassalia

# Analytical Thinking for ADVANCED LEARNERS

Grades 3–5

Emily Hollett
and
Anna Cassalia

Routledge
Taylor & Francis Group

NEW YORK AND LONDON

Cover image: © Educlips

First published 2023
by Routledge
605 Third Avenue, New York, NY 10158

and by Routledge
4 Park Square, Milton Park, Abingdon, Oxon, OX14 4RN

*Routledge is an imprint of the Taylor & Francis Group, an informa business*

© 2023 Emily Hollett and Anna Cassalia

The right of Emily Hollett and Anna Cassalia to be identified as authors of this work has been asserted in accordance with sections 77 and 78 of the Copyright, Designs and Patents Act 1988.

All rights reserved. The purchase of this copyright material confers the right on the purchasing institution to download pages which bear the Support Material icon. No other parts of this book may be reprinted or reproduced or utilised in any form or by any electronic, mechanical, or other means, now known or hereafter invented, including photocopying and recording, or in any information storage or retrieval system, without permission in writing from the publishers.

*Trademark notice*: Product or corporate names may be trademarks or registered trademarks, and are used only for identification and explanation without intent to infringe.

*Library of Congress Cataloging-in-Publication Data*
A catalog record for this title has been requested

ISBN: 978-1-032-21419-1 (hbk)
ISBN: 978-1-032-19926-9 (pbk)
ISBN: 978-1-003-26833-8 (ebk)

DOI: 10.4324/9781003268338

Typeset in Warnock Pro
by Deanta Global Publishing Services, Chennai, India

Access the Support Material: www.routledge.com/9781032199269

*We would like to dedicate this book to all the students we have taught and will teach. You are the reason why we love this profession and wrote this series. We would also like to dedicate this series to our families, who have supported us unconditionally.*

# Contents

| | | |
|---|---|---|
| Acknowledgments | | x |
| Preface | | xi |
| | Introduction to Analytical Thinking | 1 |
| | Materials | 1 |
| | Introduction: Frame of the Discipline | 1 |
| | Primary Source: Artwork Analysis | 5 |
| | Thinking Skills Avatar | 7 |
| | Bibliography | 9 |
| Chapter 1 | Sub-Skill 1: Noticing Details | 11 |
| | Noticing Details Lesson 1: Observing Details | 12 |
| | Noticing Details Lesson 2: Determining Important Details | 26 |
| | Noticing Details Authentic Application Activity: Attribute Blocks Chains | 31 |
| | Noticing Details Concluding Activities | 35 |
| | Bibliography | 37 |

# Contents

| | | |
|---|---|---|
| Chapter 2 | Sub-Skill 2: Asking Questions | 39 |
| | Asking Questions Lesson 1: Asking Questions to Determine Relationships | 40 |
| | Asking Questions Lesson 2: Writing Questions about the World | 60 |
| | Asking Questions Authentic Application Activity: Writing Nature Similes | 68 |
| | Asking Questions Concluding Activities | 70 |
| | Bibliography | 71 |
| Chapter 3 | Sub-Skill 3: Classifying and Organizing | 73 |
| | Classifying and Organizing Lesson 1: Sorting into Sets | 74 |
| | Classifying and Organizing Lesson 2: Belonging to Sub-Sets | 79 |
| | Classifying and Organizing Authentic Application Activity: Venn Diagrams and Dichotomous Keys | 87 |
| | Classifying and Organizing Concluding Activities | 105 |
| | Bibliography | 105 |
| Chapter 4 | Sub-Skill 4: Make a Hypothesis | 107 |
| | Make a Hypothesis Lesson 1: Using Observations to Make a Hypothesis | 108 |
| | Make a Hypothesis Lesson 2: Curiosity Breeds More Questions | 117 |
| | Make a Hypothesis Authentic Application Activity: Introduction to the Scientific Method | 123 |
| | Make a Hypothesis Concluding Activities | 128 |
| | Bibliography | 135 |
| Chapter 5 | Sub-Skill 5: Investigate and Reflect | 137 |
| | Investigate and Reflect Lesson 1: How Does Failure Lead to Success? | 138 |
| | Investigate and Reflect Lesson 2: Analyzing Data to Determine a Conclusion | 143 |
| | Investigate and Reflect Authentic Application Activity: Analytical Thinking Code Breaker | 148 |

## Contents

Investigate and Reflect Concluding Activities 166
Bibliography 166

Appendix A: Assessments 167
Appendix B: Extensions 181

# Acknowledgments

Special credit and acknowledgment must go to the many individuals whose work has paved the way for current educators like ourselves.

We draw great inspiration from the work of Sandra Kaplan, Tamra Stambaugh, and Joyce VanTassel-Baska, whose curricular frameworks and research into best practice for teaching gifted learners are a driving force in shaping our own work.

Our guiding principles are grounded in National Association for Gifted Children (NAGC) programming standards, and we are so thankful for this organization's tireless dedication to gifted students, advocacy, and lifelong learning.

Clipart courtesy of Educlips. Used with permission under an extended license for hard copy books.

Handout font courtesy of Kimberly Geswein. Used with permission under a single font license.

# Preface

The *Integrated Lessons in Higher Order Thinking Skills* series provides explicit instruction, targeted problems, and activities to teach gifted and high-ability students how to think using convergent, divergent, analytical, evaluative, and visual-spatial reasoning.

This unit was developed by and for teachers of gifted and advanced learners to provide explicit instruction in higher order thinking skills. In today's ever-changing, fast-paced world, our students require skill sets beyond rote memorization. Vast research supports the development of higher order thinking skills, including both creative and critical thinking skills which go beyond basic observation of facts and memorization. Systematically teaching these processes to students develops their ability to use these skills across the curriculum, building their ability to be "thinkers"—the ultimate goal of education.

The term "21st Century Thinking Skills" is widely used in education today, and while definitions vary, most educators agree: we need to be teaching our students not just *what* to think, but *how* to think. Learners in the 21st century must possess an array of thinking skills. They must be inquisitive about the world around them, and willing to ask questions and make mistakes. They must be logical and strategic thinkers. Logical thinking requires students to clarify problems while analyzing and making inferences based on the given information. Strategic, or deliberate, thinking requires students to think about where

# Preface

they are now in the learning process versus where they want to be in the future, and then determine action steps to achieve their goals.

Gifted and high-ability students require specialized instruction which is organized by key concepts and overarching themes. They need content which requires abstract thinking on a higher level than what is typically required by the general education curriculum. Beyond this, they require time to grapple with meaningful problems and derive defensible solutions. The *Integrated Lessons in Higher Order Thinking Skills* series provides scaffolded, focused lessons to teach these skills and give students authentic opportunities to develop these vital thinking processes.

## Rationale

As Tony Wagner (Wagner and Compton, 2012) noted, our current educational system is obsolete and failing to educate our youth for the world of tomorrow. Wagner (Wagner and Compton, 2012) stated, "Students who only know how to perform well in today's educational system—get good grades and test scores and earn degrees—will no longer be those who are most likely to succeed. Thriving in the twenty-first century will require real competencies far more than academic credentials" (p. 20). Our educational system must help our youth discover their passions and purpose in life, and then develop the crucial skills necessary to think critically and creatively, communicate effectively, and problem-solve (Wagner and Compton, 2012).

Developing 21st-century thinkers requires a classroom environment that welcomes cognitive discourse and embraces the growth mindset approach. We must also teach our students that it is acceptable not to have an immediate answer; that some questions have many possible solutions, and indeed, some may never be answered; that persevering and being able to admit what you don't know is an important piece of learning.

Today's students must use metacognition, or awareness of and reflection on thinking processes. Metacognitive thinking is abstract in that one must analyze their thinking processes. Examples of this type of thinking might be asking oneself: "How did I get to that answer?" or "Where did my thinking go off track?" Learning to analyze the process of thinking is vital to problem-solving and learning. Teaching metacognitive strategies is a powerful way to improve students' self-efficacy, depth of thinking, and inquiry skills.

Students of the 21st century must develop problem-solving skills which require both creative and critical thinking. Creativity is a divergent thought process which involves generating new and unique possibilities. Critical thinking is a thought process which involves examining possibilities using a systematic, constructive method. Our students will be faced with unforeseen challenges that they must be able to think about creatively, critically, and strategically to

# Preface

solve. We, as educators, cannot possibly teach students everything there is to know, as the amount of new information available in the world is multiplying rapidly. Therefore, we must teach students to be inquisitive, analytical, innovative, evaluative, and curious. Learning and applying these thinking skills will prepare our students to solve the problems of tomorrow.

While we know the importance of higher order thinking, it is often left behind the "testable subjects" such as reading, writing, and arithmetic. This series was created to merge higher order thinking skills and the academic content students must grapple with in school. Systematic instruction in higher order thinking skills coupled with rigorous academic content is a relevant and engaging method to teach the students of the 21st century.

Higher order thinking consists of several distinctive and sophisticated thought processes. Central to these processes are the areas of systematic decision making (deductive reasoning), evaluative thinking, divergent (creative) thinking, concept attainment, and rule usage (analytical). In addition, visual-spatial reasoning has emerged as one of the most important skills for developing overall academic expertise, especially in technical fields. Each of these central processes is addressed in its own book within the *Integrated Lessons in Higher Order Thinking Skills* series.

## Focus Strand: Analytical Thinking

Analytical reasoning is a unique and vital thinking skill which helps students think logically and critically about the world around them. Thinking analytically helps us to break down complex ideas into understandable bits of information. This unit is unique in that it allows students to engage in productive struggle while critically evaluating facts and developing questions to test. It encompasses the core skills and strategies of observation, categorization, inquiry, research, and logical reasoning. Working through the lessons in this book, students will learn strategies and specific academic vocabulary in five distinctive analytical thinking sub-skills, applying each of these skills to new and complex problems. The goal of this unit is to help students learn to be scientific and systematic in their approaches to researching and solving problems.

Students will learn analytical reasoning strategies in the sub-skills of noticing details, asking questions, classifying and organizing information, making hypotheses, and investigating and reflecting. Each of these skills is taught explicitly through three lessons, increasing in complexity and abstraction, and culminating in an application lesson and activity. This approach allows students to build their analytical thinking skills incrementally and apply each skill as it develops. By completing all lessons in this book, students will be able to apply analytical thinking skills and strategies to a variety of problems, situations, and contexts.

## Conceptual Framework

This curriculum is targeted for third through fifth grade gifted and high-ability students. Each of the five Thinking Skills units will provide students ways to develop problem-solving skills which require both creative and critical thinking. Frameworks for questioning and methodology were drawn from several research-based sources, including the Depth and Complexity Framework (Kaplan and Gould), The Four Question Strategy for developing scientific experiments (Cothron, Rezba, and Giese), Set Theory (Cantor), and Dichotomous Keys (Waller).

Working through the lessons in this book, students will make connections by thinking in ways that incorporate elements of the Depth and Complexity Framework, such as thinking like a disciplinarian, connecting to universal themes, reasoning using question stems derived from the icons/elements, and examining problems through the lens of the content imperatives. Students will analyze sets of information categorizing and sorting based on rules. Students will learn to categorize using the dichotomous key method, which is a series of "yes" and "no" questions to further delineate species. Students will also plan and conduct an experiment using questioning stem and the scientific method. Visual thinking routines are also incorporated to help scaffold students' metacognitive processes. Each of these research-based frameworks is embedded within the lessons in the form of question stems, instructional processes, graphic organizers, and methodology.

Each unit in the series uses explicit instruction to directly and systematically teach students how to think. Research shows that the most empirically supported method for teaching critical thinking is explicit instruction (Abrami, Bernard, Borokhovski, Wade, Surkes, Tamim, and Zhang, 2008). Using explicit instruction makes the learning outcomes clear.

Students are provided with clear, specific objectives. The unit lessons are broken down into manageable chunks of information. The teacher models the thinking skill with clear explanations and verbalizes their thinking process. Students are taught specific ways to reason and problem-solve. Students then practice the skills while the teacher provides feedback. At the conclusion of each lesson, students are asked to think metacognitively about their own learning.

## Lesson Format and Guidelines

Each *Integrated Lessons in Higher Order Thinking Skills* unit follows the same format. Students are introduced to the higher order thinking skill through

# Preface

introductory lessons and materials to build schema in the targeted thinking area addressed in the unit. The introductory lesson in each unit provides a real-world connection. The overarching thinking skill is then broken down into five sub-skills. Each sub-skill is explicitly taught in three lessons. First, the students will be introduced to the sub-skill using an anchor chart. Then, students will participate in a warm-up activity teaching the sub-skill. Next, students will read and analyze trade books which highlight the sub-skill. Finally, students will participate in an activity learning to use the sub-skill. The third lesson in each sub-skill provides an opportunity for the students to apply the sub-skill in an authentic application activity. Key features of this unit as well as lesson summaries are outlined in Table P.1.

## Unit Features

### *Materials*

Included in this book are blackline masters of consumable materials to be used with students. Student handouts are provided with each lesson, and they include reading reflections, graphic organizers, full text stories for collaborative learning activities, formative "exit tickets," and others. Teacher materials, including anchor chart posters to provide visual cues for sub-skills, detailed lesson plans, and assessment rubrics, are also included. Other needed and optional materials are listed in lesson outlines. Links are provided for online resources, such as short video clips, and are accurate at the time of this book's printing.

Throughout the unit, trade books are used to teach and explore sub-skills in familiar contexts. These carefully selected trade books provide an exemplar for the lesson's focus. The recommended books are common and easily accessible; however, alternate texts are recommended to target each sub-skill (see Appendix B). Many of the texts may also have a digital version readily available as an online read aloud, accessible through a quick internet search.

In addition, some lessons utilize common classroom manipulatives such as attribute blocks, pattern blocks, or Tangrams. Printable versions of these manipulatives are also provided as handouts where they are used.

*Teacher's note*: It is always recommended that teachers preview any content (books, videos, images, etc.) before implementing it with students. Be sure to consider the context of the classroom and/or school in which the materials are to be used, being sensitive to the needs, experiences, and diversity of the students. Where possible, alternate trade books are suggested. Links provided are known to be accurate at the time of this book's publication.

## TABLE P.1
Unit Overview

| | |
|---|---|
| **Introduction and Rationale**<br>Teacher introduction providing rationale for the unit. | ❏ Outline of Thinking Skills: Teacher reference explaining an overview of each thinking skill and outcome.<br>❏ Standards Alignment: Unit alignment to both CCSS and NAGC standards are outlined. |
| **Thinking Skill Overview**<br>This section provides introductory lessons and materials to build schema for students in the specific targeted thinking skill addressed in the unit. | ❏ Frame of the Discipline: Think Like a Researcher<br>■ Students gain understanding of authentic uses for analytical thinking skills within a career context.<br>❏ Artwork Analysis: Students analyze two pieces of classic visual art through the lens of analytical thinking to build thinking skill schema.<br>❏ Thinking Skills Avatar: Provides an ongoing touchstone for students to record key details and synthesize learning throughout the unit. |
| **Sub-Skill 1: Noticing Details**<br>In this section, students will analyze items in sets to identify, appraise, and discriminate between attributes. | ❏ Lesson 1: Observing Details<br>■ Students will identify, sort, and classify attribute blocks by similarities and differences.<br>❏ Lesson 2: Determining Important Details<br>■ Students will learn to identify essential and non-essential details and adjust thinking when sorting items based on attributes.<br>❏ Authentic Application Activity: Attribute Blocks Chains<br>■ Students will connect shapes in an attribute change chain to broaden their understanding of how objects in sets are similar and different. |
| **Sub-Skill 2: Asking Questions**<br>In this section, students will develop inquiry skills through a variety of activities that encourage them to observe and question the world around them. | ❏ Lesson 1: Asking Questions to Determine Relationships<br>■ Students will work with analogies to develop the skill of asking questions to make connections between items.<br>❏ Lesson 2: Writing Questions about the World<br>■ Students will examine items found in nature and will craft analytical questions, developing inquiry skills in a familiar context.<br>❏ Authentic Application Activity: Writing Nature Similes<br>■ Students will craft their own nature similes using the connections and questions developed in the first two lessons in this sub-skill. |

*(Continued)*

**TABLE P.1**
(Continued)

| | |
|---|---|
| **Sub-Skill 3: Classifying and Organizing** <br> In this section, students learn to group information in a meaningful manner. | ❏ Lesson 1: Sorting into Sets <br> ■ Students learn to sort and group items by rules, creating "sets" of items. <br> ❏ Lesson 2: Belonging to Sub-Sets <br> ■ Students discover the concept of sub-sets. They will practice applying this understanding to new sets and sub-sets. <br> ❏ Authentic Application Activity: Venn Diagrams and Dichotomous Keys <br> ■ Students will classify and organize information using a dichotomous key. Then they will compare the classifications using Venn diagrams. |
| **Sub-Skill 4: Make a Hypothesis** <br> Students will use notice details, ask questions, and make a prediction based on what is known. | ❏ Lesson 1: Using Observations to Make a Hypothesis <br> ■ Students will learn how both mathematicians and scientists make predictions based on observations and schema. <br> ❏ Lesson 2: Curiosity Breeds More Questions <br> ■ Students will develop a scientific investigation using the Four Question Strategy. <br> ❏ Authentic Application Activity: Introduction to the Scientific Method <br> ■ Students gain background knowledge on a scientific topic, ask a testable question, and write a hypothesis. |
| **Sub-Skill 5: Investigate and Reflect** <br> Students focus their ideas, develop and conduct an experiment, analyze data, and reflect on their findings. | ❏ Lesson 1: How Does Failure Lead to Success? <br> ■ Students will design and conduct a scientific experiment. They will collect and analyze the data gathered. <br> ❏ Lesson 2: Analyzing Data to Determine a Conclusion <br> ■ Students will draw a conclusion based on their data and share the results. <br> ❏ Authentic Application Activity: Analytical Thinking Code Breaker <br> ■ Students will use all the thinking skills learned throughout this unit to complete an escape game–style scenario. |
| **Appendix A** | ❏ Assessment Options |
| **Appendix B** | ❏ Extension Options |

# Preface

## Assessments

Possible solutions and suggested key understandings are provided throughout the unit. These sample answers were created to help the teacher see the intended purpose for each lesson and illustrate the thinking skills students should be mastering. However, due to the open-ended nature of many of the lessons and activities, these answers should only be used as a guide and variations should be encouraged.

Blackline masters of assessment options are provided in Appendix A. Formative assessments are provided throughout the unit in the form of an exit ticket to conclude each sub-skill section. An overall unit rubric is provided along with diagnostic guidelines for observation. A whole-group checklist is provided for each sub-skill with diagnostic guidelines included. Teachers should review and select assessment options that best meet their goals for their students. It is recommended that students be formatively assessed on the thinking skills as this an ongoing process and all progress should be celebrated and acknowledged.

## Time Allotment

Each lesson in this unit is intended to be taught in 60–90 minutes, but some lessons may take less or more time. In general, this unit can be taught in 15–20 hours of instructional time.

# Unit Goals and Objectives

## Concept

To develop conceptual awareness of analytical thinking skills using cross-curricular lessons, the students will:

- ❏ Learn to analyze items, identify, appraise, and discriminate between attributes
- ❏ Learn to inquire through observations and questioning
- ❏ Classify and sort information
- ❏ Make a hypothesis based on observations and questions
- ❏ Develop an understanding of how to conduct experiments

## Process

To develop analytical reasoning based on critical observation, valid evidence, and inferencing skills to determine a single correct answer, the students will:

- Identify and examine attributes learning to discern between essential and non-essential details
- Work with analogies to develop the skill of relationships
- Sort and group items by rules creating sets and sub-sets of items
- Use their skills of observing and questioning to determine a testable question and write a hypothesis
- Conduct an experiment using the scientific method

# Standards Alignment

## Common Core State Standards (CCSS)

Standards are aligned with each of the five thinking skills targeted in the series *Integrated Lessons in Higher Order Thinking Skills*. Specific thinking skills are noted using the following key (see also Table P.2):

- A: Analytical Thinking
- C: Convergent Thinking
- D: Divergent Thinking
- E: Evaluative Thinking
- V: Visual-Spatial Thinking

## NAGC Programming Standards Alignment

Teaching thinking skills aligns with NAGC programming standards as best practice for gifted students:

- **Standard 1**: Students create awareness of and interest in their learning and cognitive growth
- **Standard 2**: Thinking skill aligned assessments provide evidence of learning progress
- **Standard 3**: Explicit instruction in thinking skills and metacognitive strategies is research-based best practice and meets the needs of gifted

**TABLE P.2**
CCSS Alignment

| | | |
|---|---|---|
| Language Standards | CCR Anchor Standards for Reading<br>*1, 6, 7, 8* | ❏ Draw logical inferences from text (C/E)<br>❏ Cite text evidence to support claims (C/E)<br>❏ Assess perspectives (A/C/D/E/V)<br>❏ Evaluate various content formats (A/C/D/E/V)<br>❏ Evaluate arguments based on evidence (E) |
| | CCR Anchor Standards for Writing<br>*1, 3, 4, 8, 9, 10* | ❏ Write arguments, citing text evidence and using valid reasoning (C/E)<br>❏ Write narratives (D)<br>❏ Develop written work appropriate to a variety of tasks (A/C/D/E/V)<br>❏ Evaluate and synthesize information from a variety of sources (E)<br>❏ Draw evidence to support analysis (A)<br>❏ Write routinely and for many purposes (A/C/D/E/V) |
| | CCR Anchor Standards for Speaking and Listening<br>*1, 2, 3, 4* | ❏ Collaborate for a variety of purposes with a variety of partners (A/C/D/E/V)<br>❏ Integrate information from a variety of sources (A/C/D/E/V)<br>❏ Critically evaluate speakers' perspectives (E)<br>❏ Present information, including evidence, in ways that allow others to follow lines of reasoning (A/C/E) |
| | CCR Anchor Standards for Language<br>*3, 5, 6* | ❏ Make effective use of appropriate language in a variety of contexts (A/C/D/E/V)<br>❏ Understand and make use of figurative language (A/D/E)<br>❏ Develop and apply academic vocabulary (A/C/D/E/V) |
| Mathematics Standards | CCSS for Mathematics: Practice Standards | ❏ Make sense of problems and persevere in solving them<br>❏ Reason abstractly and quantitatively<br>❏ Construct viable arguments and critique the reasoning of others<br>❏ Model with mathematics<br>❏ Use appropriate tools strategically<br>❏ Attend to precision<br>❏ Look for and make use of structure<br>❏ Look for and express regularity in repeated reasoning<br>*Applicable to problems presented in all Thinking Skills units.* |

*(Continued)*

**TABLE P.2**
(Continued)

|  | CCSS for Mathematics: Operations and Algebraic Thinking *2.OA, 3.OA, 4.OA, 5.OA* | ❑ Generate and analyze patterns and relationships (A/C/V)<br>❑ Represent problems both concretely and abstractly (A/C/V) |
|---|---|---|
|  | CCSS for Mathematics: Measurement and Data *2.MD, 3.MD, 4.MD, 5.MD* | ❑ Represent and interpret data (A/C/V) |
|  | CCSS for Mathematics: Geometry *2.G, 3.G, 4.G, 5.G* | ❑ Solve problems involving the coordinate plane (V)<br>❑ Solve problems involving lines, angles, and dimensions (V)<br>❑ Reason with shapes and their attributes (V) |

students for opportunities to develop depth, complexity, and abstraction in thinking and inquiry
❑ **Standard 5**: Competence in thinking skills promotes cognitive, social-emotional, and psychosocial development of students

# Bibliography

Abrami, P.C., Bernard, R.M., Borokhovski, E., Wade, A., Surkes, M.A., Tamim, R., and Zhang, D. (2008). Instructional interventions affecting critical thinking skills and dispositions: A stage 1 meta-analysis. *Review of Educational Research*, 78(4), 1102–1134.

Bagaria, J. (n.d.). Set theory. In E.N. Zalta (Ed.), *The Stanford encyclopedia of philosophy* (Spring 2020 ed.). https://plato.stanford.edu/archives/spr2020/entries/set-theory/.

Common Core State Standards Initiative. (2022a) Common core state standards for mathematics. http://www.corestandards.org/wp-content/uploads/Math_Standards1.pdf.

Common Core State Standards Initiative. (2022b) Common core state standards for English language arts & literacy in history/social studies, science, and technical subjects. http://www.corestandards.org/wp-content/uploads/ELA_Standards1.pdf.

Cothron, J., Rezbra, R., and Giese, R. (2000). *Students and research*. Dubuque, IA: Kendall/Hunt Publishing Company.

Dweck, C.S. (2006). *Mindset: The new psychology of success.* New York: Random House.

Griffing, L.R. (2011). Who invented the dichotomous key? *American Journal of Botany, 98*(12), 1911–1923. https://doi.org/10.3732/ajb.1100188.

Kaplan, S. and Gould, B. (1995, 2003). *Depth & complexity icons, OERI, Javits project T.W.O. 2. Educator to educator. LVI.* J. Taylor Education, 2016.

NAGC Professional Standards Committee. (2018–2019). 2019 Pre-K-grade 12 gifted programming standards. https://www.nagc.org/sites/default/files/standards/Intro%202019%20Programming%20Standards.pdf.

Tishman, S., MacGillivray, D., and Palmer, P. (1999). Investigating the educational impact & potential of the MoMA's visual thinking curriculum. http://www.pz.harvard.edu/projects/momas-visual-thinking-curriculum-project.

Wagner, T., and Compton, R.A. (2012). *Creating innovators: The making of young people who will change the world.* New York: Scribner.

# Introduction to Analytical Thinking

## Materials

- ❏ Handout I.1: Analytical Thinking: Do It Like a Researcher! (one per student)
- ❏ Handout I.2: Framing the Thinking of a Researcher (one per student)
- ❏ Primary Source Artwork
  - ■ https://www.wikiart.org/en/maria-sibylla-merian/metamorphosis-insectorum-surinamensium-1705 (Blue Butterfly)
  - ■ https://nmwa.org/art/collection/plate-18-dissertation-insect-generations-and-metamorphosis-surinam/ (Arachnids)
- ❏ Handout I.3: Primary Source: Art Analysis (one per small group of students)
- ❏ Handout I.4: Analytical Thinking Avatar (one per student)

## Introduction: Frame of the Discipline

- ❏ Tell students they will be learning how to think using analytical reasoning. Analytical thinking involves identifying and defining a

problem, and then extracting and organizing key information and data to develop workable solutions.
- Read together Analytical Thinking: Do It Like a Researcher! (Handout I.1).
- Model answering the questions in Framing the Thinking of a Researcher (Handout I.2). Key understandings are outlined in Box I.1.

> ## Box I.1: Framing the Thinking of a Researcher Key Understandings
>
> - *What questions do researchers ask?*
>   - What is already known about this topic?
>   - What do I wonder about this topic?
>   - What would happen if…?
>   - Where can I find more information about…?
> - *What tools or thinking skills does a researcher need?*
>   - Able to notice details and be observant.
>   - Able to ask good questions.
>   - Able to conduct research using various resources.
>   - Able to classify and sort information into categories.
>   - Able to create a hypothesis.
>   - Able to conduct research experiments and draw conclusions based on facts.
> - *Why are researchers important in today's world?*
>   - Researchers are necessary to help learn about the world around us.
>   - Researchers use systematic research structures to obtain facts.
> - *How do researchers think about new information?*
>   - Researchers read relevant books, articles, websites, etc. to gather all information currently known about a topic.
>   - Researchers use this knowledge to generate new questions.
>   - Researchers make hypotheses to test.
>   - Researchers design and conduct experiments.
>   - Researchers draw conclusions based on facts.
> - *Describe the main purpose of a researcher.*
>   - Researchers enhance society by advancing the knowledge and understanding of theories, concepts, and ideas in our world.

# Handout I.1: Analytical Thinking: Do it Like a Researcher

Name: _____

Researchers are people who work to apply logical thinking to investigate an idea or solve a problem. They look at all relevant facts and information to identify patterns or trends. Sometimes, these people work in laboratories doing scientific research. Other times, college professors conduct academic research on their topic of study. One thing all researchers have in common is their ability to think in certain ways. Researchers use **analytical thinking** skills to find new information and solve problems. **Analytical thinking** means studying parts of things in order to determine a solution to a problem.

Analytic thinking involves examining what is known about a topic and building on it. The first step in analytical thinking is **NOTICING DETAILS**. This means looking at facts and theories from all different angles to see the known parts. Researchers must read relevant books, journals, websites, take notes, and draw conclusions based on what is currently known about a topic. It is important to carefully notice all the known facts on a topic.

The second step in analytical thinking is to **ASK QUESTIONS**. Researchers take the information they have studied and form new questions to ponder. This may include proving or falsifying existing theories or trying to explain current observations.

The third step in analytical thinking is **CLASSIFYING AND ORGANIZING** the new information. After the researcher gathers all the known information, they must sort the facts based on similarities. During the fourth step, the researcher will examine the information and **MAKE A HYPOTHESIS**. The hypothesis is an educated guess or working idea they will test to see if it is valid or correct.

The fifth step in analytical thinking is **INVESTIGATING AND REFLECTING** which includes conducting an investigation and interpreting data to draw a conclusion. Researchers must compare the new data to the past information. They will draw conclusions by making a statement summarizing what has been learned. The conclusion of the research is directly related to the hypothesis.

All research should be systematic, organized, and objective. Systematic means to follow specific steps in an organized manner. The research must remain objective which means the answers must be based on observed and measured data and facts. Conclusions should be made on facts and not opinions.

# Handout I.2: Framing the Thinking of a Researcher

Name: _____

| What questions do researchers ask? | What thinking skills or tools does a researcher need? |
|---|---|
| | |

Describe the main purpose of a researcher.

| Why are researchers important in today's world? | How do researchers think about new information? |
|---|---|
| | |

# Introduction to Analytical Thinking

❏ Tell students that throughout this unit they will be developing the skills of observation, inquiry, classification, and learning the scientific process.

## Primary Source: Artwork Analysis

❏ Display each piece of artwork, one at a time, in a format that allows students to consider the detail, color, technique, and overall impression of each. Links to digitized versions of each piece of artwork are provided in the materials section, and it is recommended that the artwork be projected or enlarged to allow students to view it clearly.
❏ Distribute the Primary Source: Art Analysis (Handout I.3).
❏ Tell students that these illustrations were created by Maria Sibylla Merian, a German artist who lived from 1647 to 1717. Merian was fascinated by insects. She drew many such illustrations about her observations of caterpillars, butterflies, spiders, and plants. Along with each of her illustrations, she included descriptions and observations about the life cycles of these insects. Merian is credited as being one of the most significant contributors to the field of entomology, the study of insects. She was also a naturalist and botanist. Her illustrations were prized as very accurate representations of the natural world. As you look at her artwork, think like a researcher and answer the analysis questions on Handout I.3.
❏ Guide students through answering each section on the page. Key understandings are outlined in Box I.2.

## Box I.2: Primary Source: Artwork Analysis Key Understandings

❏ *Describe what you see in detail.*
  - Hand-colored illustrations of butterflies and spiders
  - Realistic insects and foliage
  - Shadings to depict depth
❏ *What can we learn from this artwork?*
  - Insect life cycles
  - Insect body parts

# Handout I.3: Primary Source: Art Analysis

Name: _____

Look carefully at the two pieces of artwork by Maria Sibylla Merian, a German artist, who lived from 1647-1717. Merian was fascinated by insects. She observed and drew many illustrations of caterpillars, butterflies, spiders, and plants. Along with each of her illustrations, she included descriptions and observations about the life cycles of these insects. Merian was one of the first entomologists, someone who studies insects. She was also a naturalist, and botanist. Her illustrations were prized as very accurate representations of the natural world. As you look at her artwork, think like a researcher and answer the questions below.

Describe what you see in detail.

What can we learn from this artwork?

Describe how Maria Sibylla's illustrations differ from the actual insects.

How can art be used as an observation tool?

- *Describe how Merian's illustrations are different from actual insects.*
  - Her illustrations were based on her observations; she then recreated two-dimensional representations, and the real insects are three-dimensional.
  - Merian may miss tiny details that could be noticed if observing an insect under a microscope.
- *How can art be used as an observation tool?*
  - Artists often have a great eye for noticing particular details which they represent in their art.
  - In Merian's time, people could look at her art to learn about insects that they weren't able to see in real life.

- Remind students they are using analytical thinking skills when they notice details by looking closely at the illustrations. Through asking questions and describing the illustrations, they are investigating and reflecting on the artwork.

## Thinking Skills Avatar

- The final introductory lesson involves students creating their own Analytical Thinking Avatar. Today, students will decorate their Avatar. Distribute Handout I.4.
- Discuss with students the concept of an avatar. An avatar is a symbolic representation of a person that can be used as a stand-in. As you move through the analytical thinking sub-skills in this unit, this page will serve as a touch point for students to connect the skills together into one representation of analytical thinking.
- Explain that throughout this unit they will be introduced to five learning targets:
  - Noticing Details
  - Asking Questions
  - Classifying and Organizing
  - Make a Hypothesis
  - Investigate and Reflect

# Handout I.4: I am an ANALYTICAL THINKER when I...

Name: _____

**CREATE YOUR ANALYTICAL THINKING AVATAR.**

**NOTICE DETAILS LIKE:**

**ASK QUESTIONS LIKE:**

**CLASSIFY & ORGANIZE LIKE:**

**MAKE A HYPOTHESIS LIKE:**

**INVESTIGATE & REFLECT LIKE:**

# Introduction to Analytical Thinking

- ❏ As students complete each target learning skill, they will pause and reflect on the key details of each sub-skill. Use the sub-skill boxes to record the keys ideas and/or illustrate a new avatar using the newly learned skill. This is a time for the students to synthesize their learning.
- ❏ Allow students time to illustrate their avatar (the outline in the top left box) to represent an analytical thinking character/avatar of their choice. The other five boxes will remain empty for now, being filled in as students complete each sub-skill in the unit.

## Bibliography

Merian, M.S. (1705). Metamorphosis Insectorum Surinamensium [hand-colored engraving on paper]. Wiki Art Visual Encyclopedia. https://www.wikiart.org/en/maria-sibylla-merian/metamorphosis-insectorum-surinamensium-1705

Merian, M.S. (1719). Plate 18 from Dissertation in Insect Generations and Metamorphosis in Surinam [hand-colored engraving on paper]. National Museum of Women in the Arts. https://nmwa.org/art/collection/plate-18-dissertation-insect-generations-and-metamorphosis-surinam/

# CHAPTER 1

# Sub-Skill 1
## *Noticing Details*

**TABLE 1.1**
Noticing Details Sub-Skills Overview

| | Thinking Skill Outline |
|---|---|
| **Focus Questions** | ❏ What do you see?<br>❏ What can we notice?<br>❏ What might be important? |
| **Lesson 1** | *Observing Details*<br>❏ **Trade Book Focus:** *Spot, the Cat* by Henry Cole<br>❏ **Practice Activity:** Identifying Attributes |
| **Lesson 2** | *Determining Important Details*<br>❏ **Trade Book Focus:** *The Jewel Fish of Karnak* by Graeme Base<br>❏ **Practice Activity:** Sorting by Attributes |
| **Authentic Application Activity** | *Attribute Block Chains*<br>❏ Make a Change Chain<br>❏ Make a Change Connecting Chain |

# ANALYTICAL THINKING for Advanced Learners, Grades 3–5

## Noticing Details Lesson 1: Observing Details

**Objective:** Carefully observe details to determine various attributes and important traits.

### *Materials*

- Handout 1.1: Noticing Details Anchor Chart (one enlarged copy for the class)
- Figure 1.1.a: Picture Poster 1 (project using document camera, or enlarge for whole class viewing)
- Figure 1.1.b: Picture Poster 2 (project using document camera, or enlarge for whole class viewing)
- Handout 1.2.a: Noticing Details Answer Sheet 1 (one per student)
- Handout 1.2.b: Noticing Details Answer Sheet 2 (one per student)
  - *Teacher's note*: Make back-to-back copies of pages 1.2.a and 1.2.b and cut them in half. Students should have a half sheet of paper with Handout 1.2.a on one side and Handout 1.2.b on the other.
- *Spot, the Cat* by Henry Cole (teacher's copy)
- Handout 1.3: Read Aloud Reflection (one per student)
- Commercial sets of attribute blocks (one for modeling, or several sets for students to share)
- Handout 1.4: Paper version of attribute blocks (duplicate as needed)
- Handout 1.5: Sorting attribute blocks—two pages (duplicate back-to-back)

### *Whole Group Introduction*

- Introduce the analytical thinking skill of noticing details. Ask for volunteers to share what they think this means. What are details? What does it mean to notice details?
- Share the Noticing Details Anchor Chart (Handout 1.1). Tell students that when they notice details, they are looking at all the attributes, characteristics, and important traits of a subject.

**Handout 1.1:** Noticing Details Anchor Chart

# NOTICING DETAILS

## LOOKING FOR ATTRIBUTES AND IMPORTANT TRAITS

# Handout 1.2.a: Noticing Details

Name: _____
Date: _____

Write down all the items you can remember from Picture Poster ~1

# Handout 1.2.a: Noticing Details

Name: _____
Date: _____

Write down all the items you can remember from Picture Poster ~1

## Handout 1.2.b: Noticing Details

Name: _____
Date: _____

Circle the items that were on Picture Poster ~2

Umbrella

Purse

Cheese

Books

Button

Cup

Band-aid

Slide

Tree

Notebook

## Handout 1.2.b: Noticing Details

Name: _____
Date: _____

Circle the items that were on Picture Poster ~2

Umbrella

Purse

Cheese

Books

Button

Cup

Band-aid

Slide

Tree

Notebook

**Figure 1.1a** Noticing Details Picture Poster 1

**Figure 1.1b** Noticing Details Picture Poster 2

- ❏ Tell students that today they will play a quick game to see how well they notice details. Preface the activity, saying something like, "In just a moment, I am going to show you a picture for 30 seconds. I want you to try and notice all the details in this picture."
- ❏ Hand out the paper so that the Noticing Details Answer Sheet 1 (Handout 1.2.a) is facing up. Tell students they are *not to pick up a pencil* until you give them permission.
- ❏ Show students the Noticing Details Picture Poster 1 (Figure 1.1.a) for 30 seconds, telling them to carefully observe everything in the picture. (It is recommended that you share this in a large format, such as in an enlarged copy or via projector using a document camera).
- ❏ Hide the scene. Tell students they may now pick up their pencil and write down every item they remember on Handout 1.2a. At the end of 2 minutes, tell students to put their pencils down.
- ❏ Show the students the Noticing Details Picture Poster 1 (Figure 1.1.a) again. Ask students to explain how they went about memorizing the items. What stood out? What made certain items easier to remember?
- ❏ Tell students they will do this activity one more time. This time, students will begin by keeping their handout with the Noticing Details Picture Poster 1 side facing up. Remind students that they will have 30 seconds to memorize all the items on Noticing Details Picture Poster 2 (Figure 1.1.b).
- ❏ Show Picture Poster 2 (Figure 1.1.b) for 30 seconds, and then hide the image.
- ❏ At this time, the students will turn over their paper so that the Noticing Details Answer Sheet 2 (Handout 1.2.b) side is showing. They will have 1 minute to circle all the items that were present on Picture Poster 2 (Figure 1.1.b).
- ❏ At the end of 1 minute, tell students to put their pencils down. Ask students to share what they circled. Show students the Noticing Details Picture Poster 2 (Figure 1.1.b).

- ❏ Ask students:
  - What items did you circle that weren't on the poster?
  - Why do you think you circled that?
  - Why did your brain do that?
- ❏ Tell students they were just practicing noticing details. Point out that many people will circle books even though they are not on the poster. Tell students that our brains naturally categorize what we observe. Our brains look to create order. On Noticing Details Picture Poster 2, all the items were related to school, so our brains naturally added books to the list. This is called a false memory; our brains naturally look for order and will make us believe we saw things that did not really occur.
- ❏ This is a great example of why it is important to really focus on noticing details.

### Read Aloud Activity

- ❏ Share the book *Spot, the Cat*, by Henry Cole. This wordless picture book shows a day in the life of Spot, the cat. He sneaks away from home and explores the city. His beloved owner is looking for Spot, and just misses him every time... As you "read," pause to find Spot on each page.
- ❏ Ask students probing questions, such as:
  - Why was it challenging to find Spot?
  - What would we notice if we really took our time to look?
  - What details exist all around us?
- ❏ Distribute the Read Aloud Reflection page (Handout 1.3). Direct students to carefully consider and answer the questions on the top half. When students have finished, discuss responses as a whole group. Then allow students time to draw a new scene for *Spot, the Cat*. Key understandings for the read aloud are outlined in Box 1.1.

## Handout 1.3: Read Aloud Reflection
*Spot the Cat* by Henry Cole

Name: _____

| Summarize the main idea of the story. | How did noticing details help you "read" this story? |

Draw a new scene for Spot the Cat. What details will you include to show what the cat is doing?

## Box 1.1: *Spot, the Cat*, Key Understandings

❏ *Summarize the main idea of the story.*
  ■ Spot, the cat, goes on a journey to explore the city by himself. When his owner notices, he frantically searches the busy city to find his cat. The boy never finds Spot but is pleasantly surprised to find him back at home.
❏ *How does noticing details help you "read" the story?*
  ■ We must look carefully at each picture to find out where Spot is.
  ■ The illustrations allow the reader to engage as a participant, noticing the items and details in each picture just as the boy is doing.
❏ *Draw a new scene for* Spot, the Cat. *What details will you include to show what the cat is doing?*
  ■ Encourage students to add many details for the "reader" to notice.

### Skill Development Activity

*Teacher's note*: You will need some attribute blocks for this lesson; if you don't have commercial attribute blocks available, you can use the blackline master provided on Handout 1.4. Students will need to color the shapes according to the colors indicated on the handout. Tell students the *thin* shapes have a fine border line, and the *thick* shapes are represented by a thick border line.

❏ To begin this lesson, let the kids do a free sort. Tell them to sort the shapes any way they'd like, but emphasize that each category must follow a rule. See what creative ways they can sort the shapes. Prompt students to look for multiple ways to sort the attribute blocks.
❏ Ask students what the four attributes are that they've noticed about the blocks. Continue prompting until students notice all four different attributes' size, color, shape, and thickness.
❏ Distribute the Sorting by Attributes page (Handout 1.5). Tell students to study the top grid. (You may want to model using a set of commercial attribute blocks and a document camera.) Ask students to explain the "rules" of this grid. Upper left: blue squares; Upper right: not blue squares; bottom left: blue not squares; bottom right: not blue and not squares.

# Handout 1.4: Attribute Blocks

Name: _____

Attribute Blocks differ in 4 ways: shape, color, size, and thickness.
**Shape:** circle, rectangle, square, triangle, hexagon
**Color:** blue, red, yellow
**Size:** big or small
**Thickness:** Thick or thin

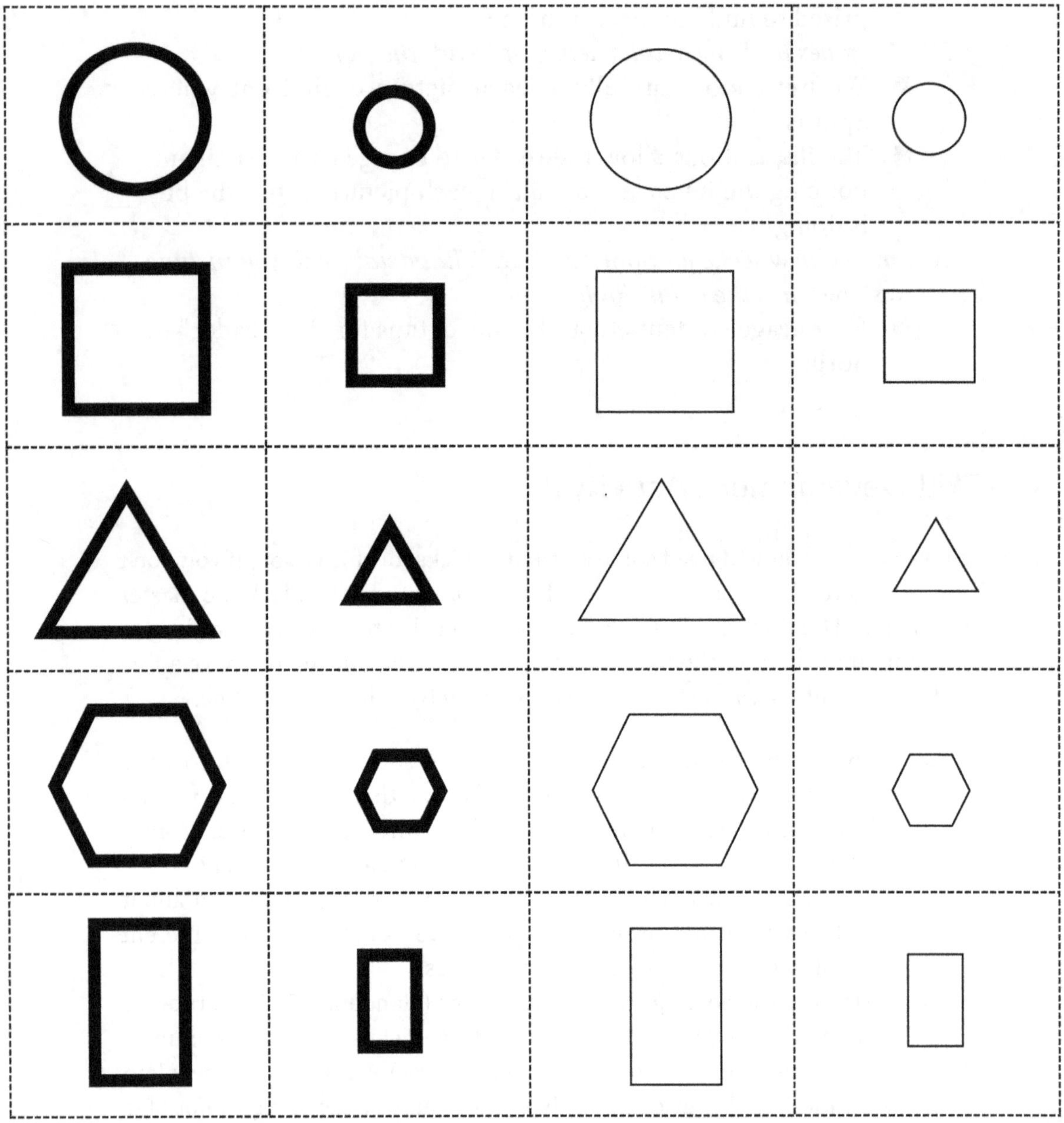

# Handout 1.5: Attribute Blocks

Name: _____

Study the diagram below. What are the rules for each quadrant?

|  | **BLUE** | **NOT BLUE** |
|---|---|---|
| **SQUARE** | B, B (squares) | Y (thick), R (squares) |
| **NOT SQUARE** | B (triangle, thin), B (circle, thick) | R (triangle), Y (hexagon) |

---

Place two block in each category. You may either glue down the attribute cards or trace attribute blocks. If you trace, make sure to color the shape and designate if it's THINK or thin.

|  | **YELLOW** | **NOT YELLOW** |
|---|---|---|
| **CIRCLE** |  |  |
| **NOT CIRCLE** |  |  |

# Handout 1.5, continued: Attribute Blocks

Name: _____

Place two block in each category. You may either glue down the attribute cards or trace attribute blocks. If you trace, make sure to color the shape and designate if it's THINK or thin.

|  | **THICK** | **THIN** |
|---|---|---|
| **RED** | | |
| **NOT RED** | | |

Place two blocks in each section, DO NOT LABEL the categories. Then give it to a neighbor, see if they can determine the four categories.

|  | _____ | _____ |
|---|---|---|
| | | |
| | | |

## TABLE 1.2
Naming the Shapes by All Four Attributes

|  | blue | not blue |
|---|---|---|
| **square** | big, blue, thin, square<br>small, blue, thin, square | big, yellow, thick, square<br>small, red, think, square |
| **not square** | small, blue, thick, triangle<br>big, blue, thick, circle | big, red, thin, triangle<br>small, yellow, thin, hexagon |

## TABLE 1.3
Visual of Just the Top of the Matrix

|  | blue | not blue |
|---|---|---|
| **square** | B  B | Y  R |

- ❏ Ask students to describe the shapes inside the section using all four attributes. See Table 1.2 for an example.
- ❏ Option for differentiation: If the whole chart is too overwhelming for your student population, begin by explaining the matrix box by box. Display Table 1.3, but cover up the right column (not blue). Explain that a matrix is used by looking at the headings along the side and top. Along the left side, they will see the heading *square*, and along the top, the first heading states *blue*; therefore, the shapes in this box are blue squares.
- ❏ Next uncover the right column. Explain that in a matrix, the left heading (square) extends to the second column (not blue); therefore, the shapes in this box are not blue squares.
- ❏ Follow the same procedure to explain how the top headings also extend to the bottom row.
- ❏ Students will complete the remaining grids either independently or with a partner. Remind students they must add at least two attribute blocks to each square.
- ❏ *Challenge*: On the last grid, students will get to create the rules. Allow students to trade papers with a partner and solve each other's grids.

# Noticing Details Lesson 2: Determining Important Details

**Objective:** Learn which details are important and which will lead you astray.

## Materials

- Computer and projector to share the Riddles Video:
  - https://www.youtube.com/watch?v=yBPraaPfLSA
- *The Jewel Fish of Karnak* by Graeme Base (teacher's copy)
- Handout 1.6: Read Aloud Reflection (one per student)
- Attribute blocks or pre-made and colored copies of Handout 1.4 (one set per student or partner pair)
- Handout 1.7: Make a Change Chain (one per student or partners)
- Handout 1.8: Make a Change Grid (one per student or partners)

## Whole Group Introduction

- Share the video on kid riddles. Tell the students they will have to notice *all* the details to solve these riddles. Project the "10 Fun Kiddy Riddles That Stump Most Adults" referenced in the materials.
- After each riddle, pause the video and ask students:
  - What details helped you solve the riddle?
  - Did any detail lead you astray, or off track?

## Read Aloud Activity

- Tell students they will be solving a riddle-like trick in the book *The Jewel Fish of Karnak*. (Tell students if they have solved this puzzle before to please not share the answers, as this would ruin the fun for everyone else.)
- Read aloud *The Jewel Fish of Karnak* by Graeme Base all the way through one time. Allow students an opportunity to carefully observe each picture.
- After you finish reading, ask students what details they noticed along the way. How might those details help in solving the riddle?
- Distribute Handout 1.6. To solve the mystery, the students will need to go back through noticing all the details and determining which details are important in solving the mystery. They should record their findings on the Read Aloud Reflection page (Handout 1.6).
- If you have multiple copies of the book, allow students to work in groups to decipher the clues. See Box 1.2 for an outline of the book's clues.

# Handout 1.6: Read Aloud Reflection
*The Jewel Fish of Karnak by Graeme Base*

Name: _____

**Clue 1**

**Clue 2**

**Clue 3**

**Clue 4**

> ### Box 1.2: *The Jewel Fish of Karnak* Clues
>
> If you choose to walk the students through the mystery, here are the main clues they will need:
>
> 1. The first clue is on the first page of the story. At the bottom there is a hieroglyphics/alphabet code key. The students may use this key to read the hieroglyphic clues throughout the story. Most of these are just random details.
> 2. The second clue is on page 24. Look at the hieroglyphics in the oval cartouche. Tell students that a cartouche was used to write important text. This one says "FRONT COVER," which tells the students to look carefully at the front cover.
> 3. The third clue is on the front cover; notice the fish's tail symbol.
> 4. The fourth clue is on page 22. Find the fish that has the same circle with a dot symbol on the tail.
> 5. To solve the puzzle, go to the back cover and turn the fish dials to the correct color pattern; this will reveal three symbols. If the students are interested, take them to http://graemebase.com.au/the-jewel-fish-of-karnak-game/ and they can enter all the information to receive a prize from the Pharaoh.

- ❏ Conclude the lesson by asking students which details were important in solving the mystery. Which details were not important? Why would the author put the extra details in the story?

### *Skill Development Activity*

- ❏ Students will continue exploring with attribute blocks. These activities will require students to notice the details and adjust their thinking.
- ❏ Have students sit in a circle. Inside the circle, put out a set of the attribute blocks. Tell students you are going to make a train; you are the first person on the train. To join the train, they must pick a block that is *one* attribute different from the person who got on in front of them. Remind students that the four attributes are color, shape, size, and thickness.

# Sub-Skill 1

One at a time, allow each student to pick an attribute block and provide feedback as to how many attributes they have changed. If they have only changed one attribute from the previous block, then they may "board the train." Guide students on picking a block which will allow them to board the train.

❏ Distribute the Make a Change Chain page (Handout 1.7) to students. Tell students they will be following the same rule—"change only one attribute"—to make an attribute chain on a paper. They will begin with a small, red, thin, square in the first box. Ask students to hold up an attribute block that could go in the next box. Discuss how there are a few correct answers, as they could change only one of the attributes of color, shape, size, or thickness.

❏ Allow students time to work with the attribute blocks and put blocks in the other squares so that each block is different in only one way from the previous block. Circulate amongst the students and ask probing questions to those who have gone astray. Once you have checked the work of the students, then allow them to either trace, color, and label thickness, or glue the appropriate attribute blocks down. If this activity is challenging, you may allow students to work in partners. See Figure 1.2 for a possible solution.

❏ Next, distribute the Making a Change Grid (Handout 1.8). Have students color the shapes according to the provided instructions and then cut them out. Tell students on this grid they will make one change going across the rows and down the columns. First, look at the attribute blocks already on the page. Ask students:
  ■ How can we use the known attribute blocks to help us fill in the rest?
  ■ Guide students to see that they know row one already has a red circle, row two has a yellow triangle, and row three has a blue rectangle.
  ■ Based on that information, what shape should go in the second box of the top row? It must be a red triangle, because that would be a change of shape from circle to triangle for the top row, and the middle column keeps the same shape but changes the color.

❏ If students seem to understand the process, allow them to proceed with a partner or individually. If students are struggling, continue asking guiding questions. See Figure 1.3 for a solution guide.

# Handout 1.7: Make a Change Chain

Name: _____

Make a Change Chain: Place a small, red, thin square in the first circle. As you move to the next, change ONLY ONE attribute. Trace and color the shapes.

# Sub-Skill 1

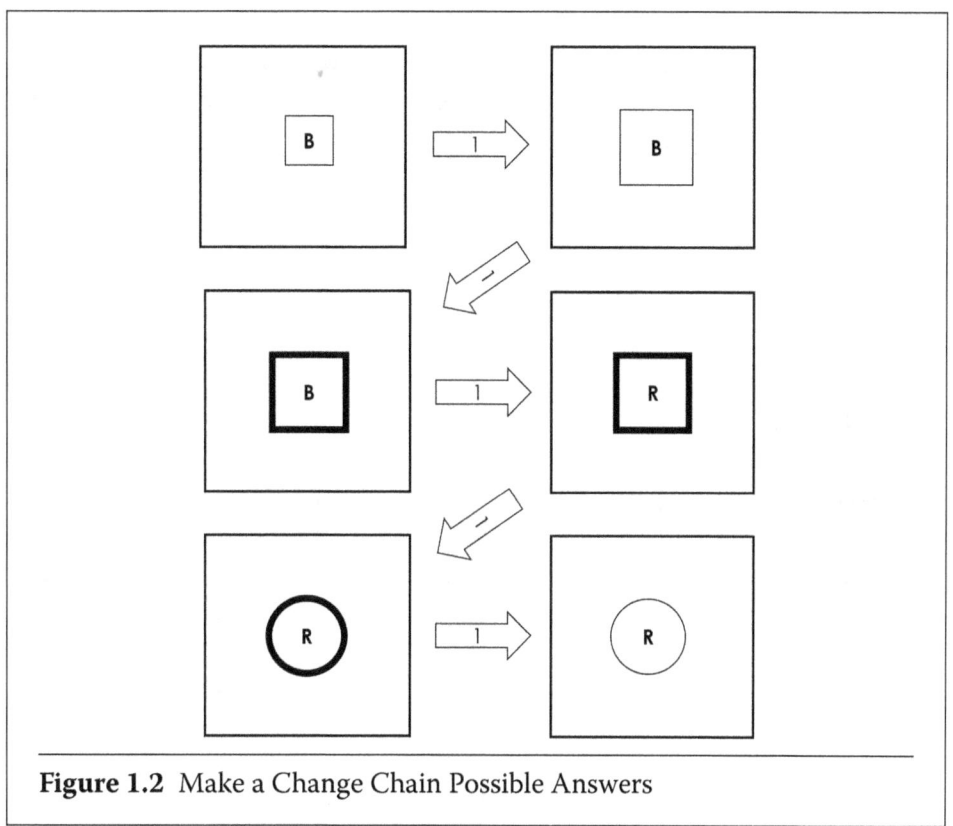

Figure 1.2 Make a Change Chain Possible Answers

## Noticing Details Authentic Application Activity: Attribute Blocks Chains

**Objective:** Determine the correct details to complete a complex chain.

### Materials

- Attribute blocks or paper versions of attribute blocks
- Handout 1.9: Making a Complex Change Chain (one story per student)
- Handout 1.10: Make a Connecting Chain (one per student)

### Authentic Application

- Have students sit in a circle. Inside the circle put out all the attribute blocks. Tell students they are going to make an attribute train again, but this time it will be a little more difficult. They will need to change either one, two, or three attributes from the previous passenger to board the train. As you are going around the circle, show either one, two, or three fingers. The student will then need to change that many attributes to

SUPPORT MATERIAL

# Handout 1.8: Make a Change Grid

Name: ______________________________________________

Make a Change GRID: As you go across the rows and down the columns the attribute blocks should have one difference. Cut and sort the attribute shapes accordingly.

Make 1 change

Make 1 change

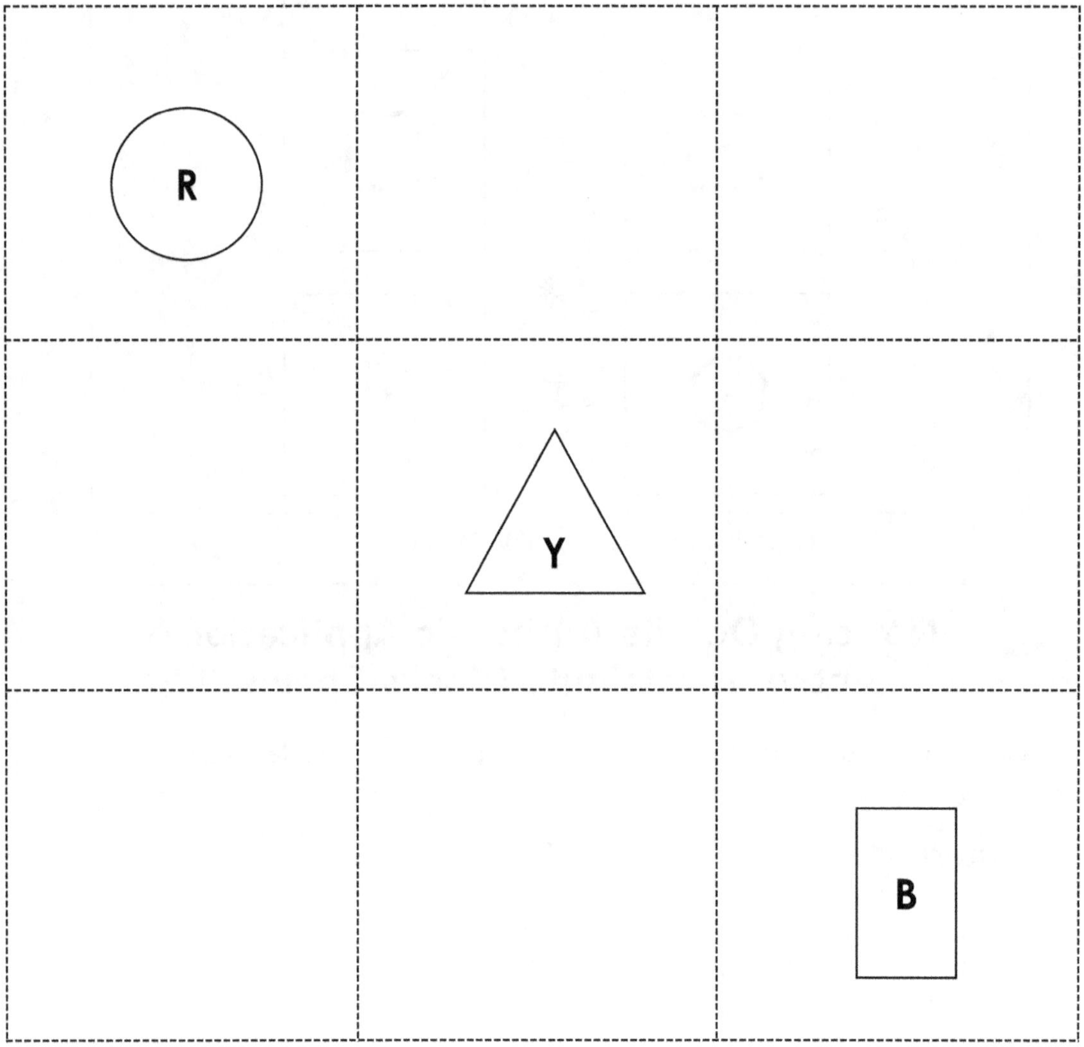


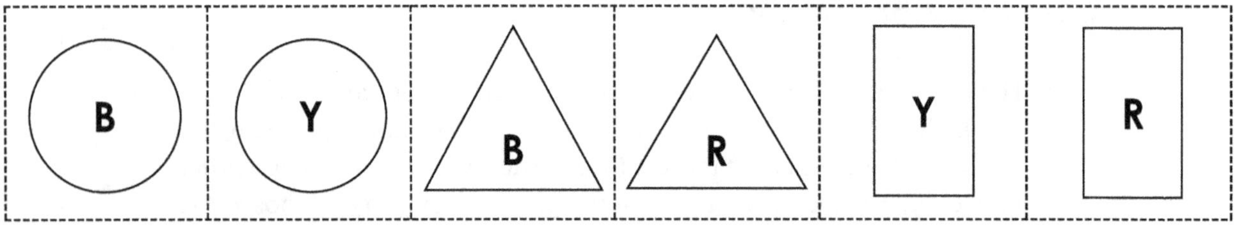

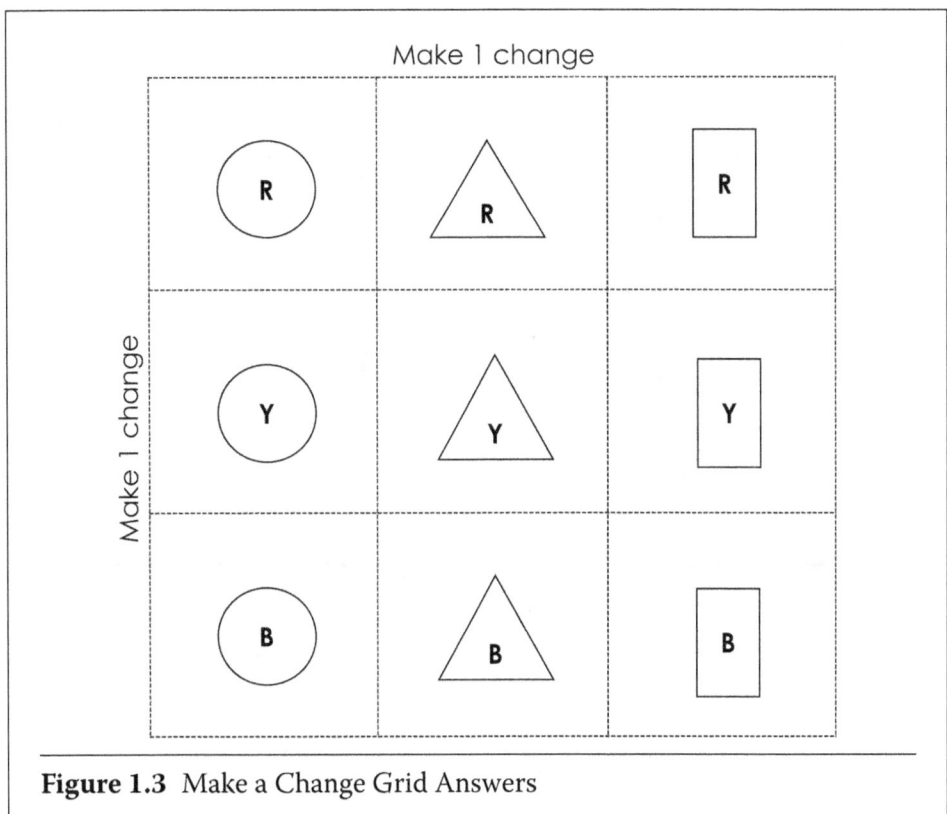

**Figure 1.3** Make a Change Grid Answers

board the train. Guide students who are struggling through prompting questions.
❏ Show students the Make a Complex Change Chain page (Handout 1.9). This follows the same procedure as before, but this time the number of attribute changes differs from box to box. You may need to model doing this one time before giving it to students. See Figure 1.4 for one possible solution.
❏ If students are comfortable with the Make a Complex Change Chain, allow them to try the Make a Change Connecting Chain (Handout 1.10). This is a circular chain in which the last shape needs to fit with the first shape. Allow students to have that cognitive struggle and encourage those showing perseverance. See Figure 1.5 for one possible solution.

Conduct a class discussion on the following questions:

❏ How does noticing details impact our lives?
❏ How do you know what details are important?
❏ What are *attributes*?

# Handout 1.9: Make a Complex Change Chain

Name: _____

Make a Change Chain: Place a blue thick, big, circle in the first box. As you move to the next, change the designated number of attributes. Trace and color the shapes.

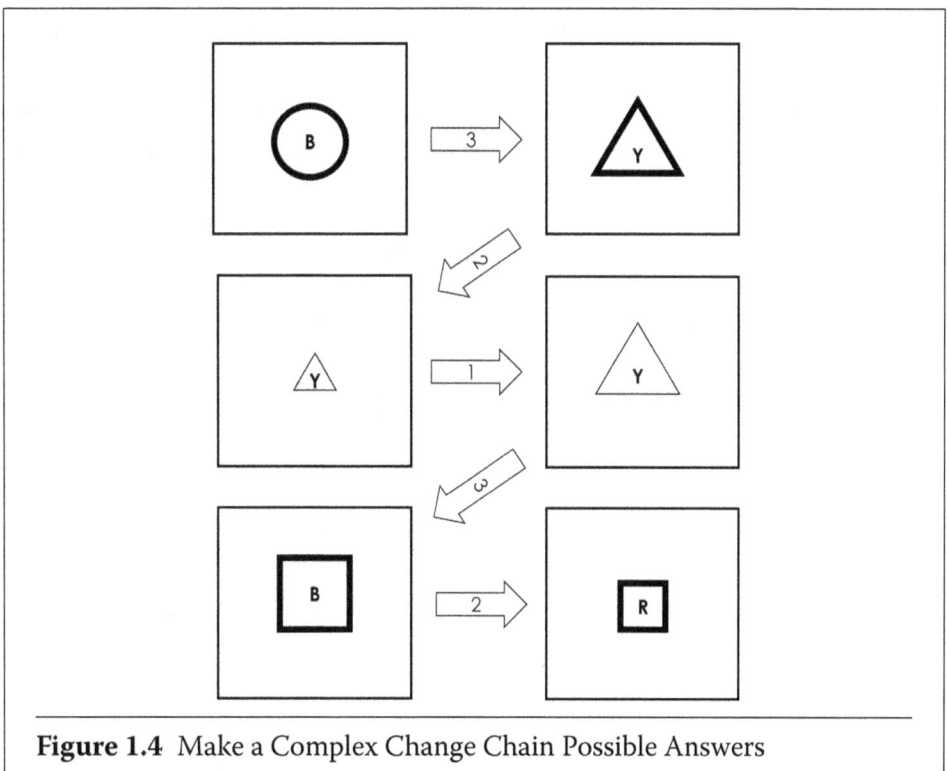

**Figure 1.4** Make a Complex Change Chain Possible Answers

## Noticing Details Concluding Activities

❏ Distribute the Noticing Details Exit Ticket (Appendix A) Ask students to reflect on their learning about the skill of noticing details in the world. Allow time for students to complete the exit ticket. Use this as a formative assessment, to gain a better understanding of your students' readiness to effectively practice the skill.
❏ If desired, complete the Group Noticing Details Rubric (Appendix A) to track students' progress with the skill.
❏ If desired, use the Analytical Thinking Student Observation Rubric (Appendix A) to assess and quantify individual students' mastery.
❏ Ask students to retrieve their Analytical Thinking Avatar (Handout I.4). In the Noticing Details box, they should either write the main ideas of this section or illustrate their avatar using the skill of noticing details.

# Handout 1.10: Make a Connecting Chain

Name: _____

Make a connecting change chain: As you go around the chain, change the attributes accordingly. Trace, color and label the attribute blocks.

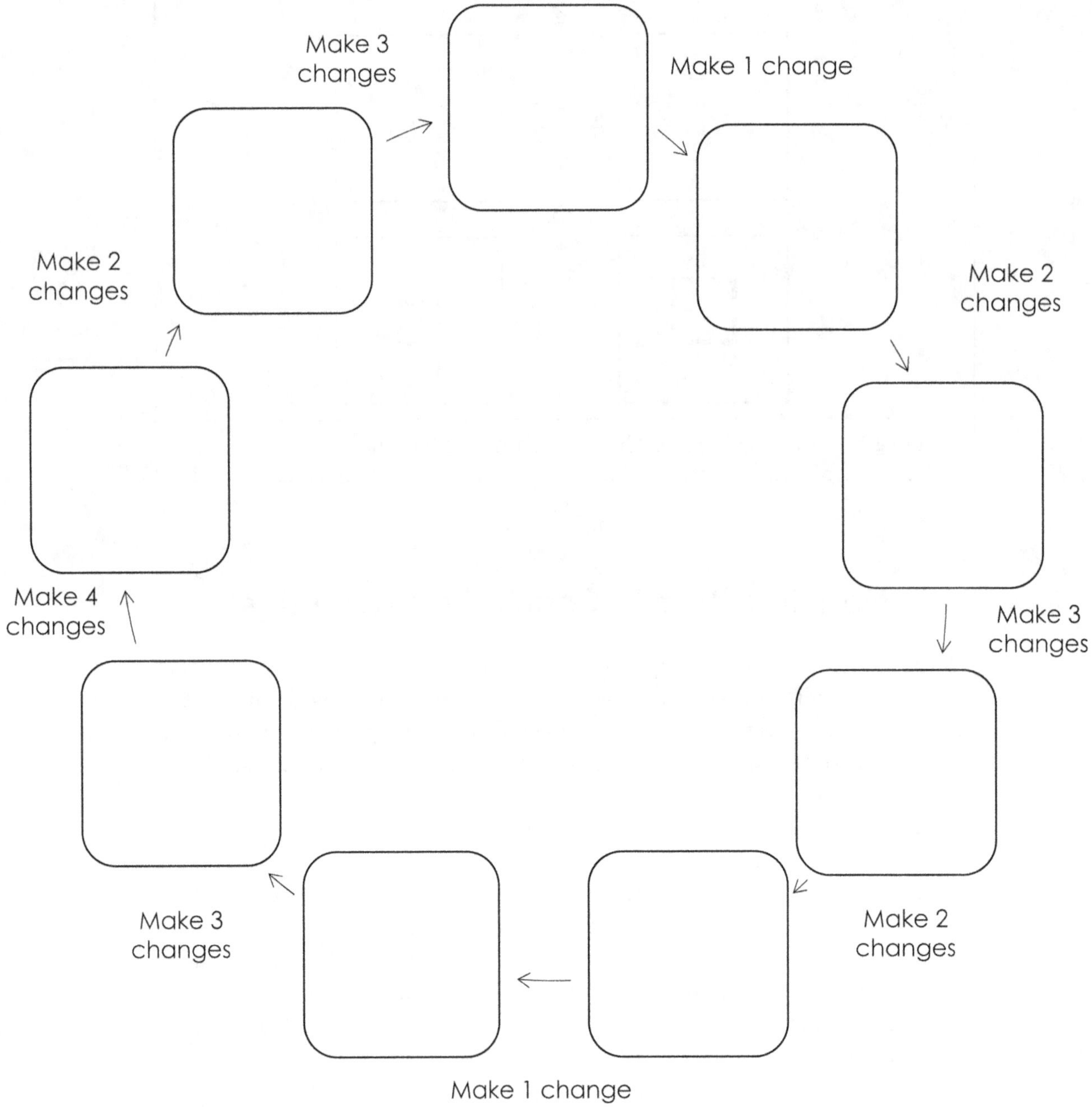

Make 3 changes

Make 1 change

Make 2 changes

Make 3 changes

Make 2 changes

Make 1 change

Make 3 changes

Make 4 changes

Make 2 changes

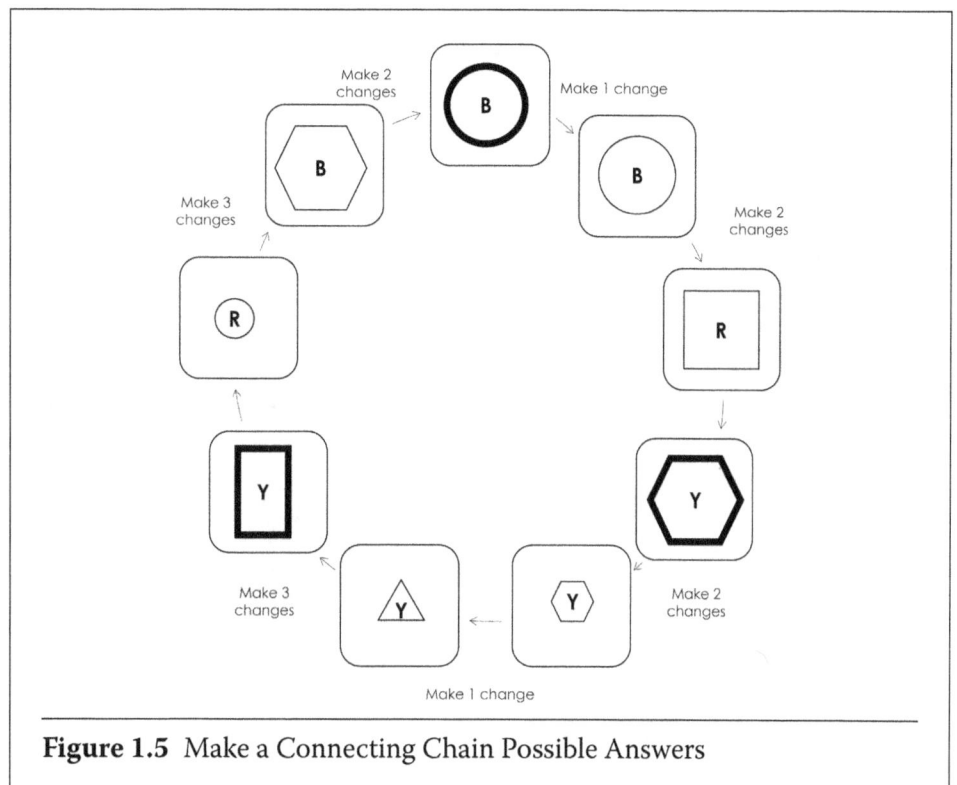

**Figure 1.5** Make a Connecting Chain Possible Answers

# Bibliography

Base, G. (2011). *The jewel fish of Karnak.* New York: Abrams Books for Young Readers.

Base, G. (2022). Solution to the cat Pharoah's challenge. *Graeme base.* http://graemebase.com.au/the-jewel-fish-of-karnak-game/.

The Bright Side. (June 25, 2018). 10 fun kiddy riddles that stump most adults. [video]. https://www.youtube.com/watch?v=yBPraaPfLSA.

Cole, H. (2016). *Spot, the cat.* New York: Little Simon Publishing.

# CHAPTER 2

# Sub-Skill 2

## *Asking Questions*

**TABLE 2.1**
Asking Questions Sub-Skill Overview

| | Thinking Skill Outline |
|---|---|
| **Focus Questions** | ❑ How can we think about this?<br>❑ What do we wonder?<br>❑ How are things alike and different? |
| **Lesson 1** | *Asking Questions to Determine Relationships*<br><br>❑ **Trade Book Focus:** *Animalogies: Animal Analogies* by Marianne Collins Berkes<br>❑ **Practice Activity:** Types of Analogies |
| **Lesson 2** | *Writing Questions about the World*<br><br>❑ **Trade Book Focus:** *Why?* by Lindsay Camp and Tony Ross<br>❑ **Practice Activity:** Nature Wonderings |
| **Authentic Application Activity** | *Writing Nature Similes*<br><br>❑ **Trade Book Focus:** *Quick as a Cricket* by Audrey Wood<br>❑ **Practice Activity:** Writing Nature Similes |

# Asking Questions Lesson 1: Asking Questions to Determine Relationships

**Objective:** Observe the world around you and ask questions.

## Materials

- Device to display short video clip: "Forky Asks a Question"
    - https://www.youtube.com/watch?v=4e4UKAOgk_k&list=PLc-UfGbMhhShgWau-Zd4Un1TmNa29jSuQ&index=2
- Handout 2.1: Asking Questions Anchor Chart (one enlarged copy for the class)
- *Animalogies: Animal Analogies* by Marianne Collins Berkes (teacher's copy)
- Handout 2.2: Read Aloud Reflection (one per student)
- Handout 2.3: Types of Analogies Mini-Book (one per student)
- Handout 2.4: Complete the Analogies (one per student)
- Handout 2.5: "I Have, Who Has?" Cards (one set for the class)

## Whole Group Introduction

- Show students the clip "Forky Asks a Question." This short clip is a funny way to introduce questioning. Forky has questions about everything.
- Ask students what they noticed about Forky. Tell students that asking questions is a wonderful way to learn about the world.
- Introduce the skill of asking questions to the students. Show the Asking Questions Anchor Chart (Handout 2.1), pointing out that questioning goes beyond the who, what, when, where, why, and how. Questioning also requires students to wonder about the world around them.
- Remind students that analytical thinkers look for things that spark curiosity and make them wonder about the world around them. Often these are unanswered questions that the thinker may want to further investigate. Ask students to generate a few "I wonder" statements about a familiar topic, such as outer space, the weather, or the seasons. Tell students that analytical thinkers also wonder about how things are related.

**Handout 2.1:** Asking Questions Anchor Chart

# ASKING QUESTIONS

## WONDERING ABOUT OUR WORLD

❏ Teach students the game "Relationship." You will say two words and ask the students: How are they alike or related?
  - Pig and cow
  - Pencil and marker
  - Sock and shoe
  - Tree and bird

## Read Aloud Activity

❏ Begin the read aloud *Animalogies: Animal Analogies* by Marianne Collins Berkes.
❏ Read the book once through just for fun.
❏ Tell students this book uses analogies which compare and contrast different things to show how they are related to each other. To write analogies you must ask yourself the question: How are these things related? Re-read the story, pausing to discuss how the animals are related in each analogy.
❏ Distribute the Read Aloud Reflection page (Handout 2.2). Direct students to carefully consider and answer the questions. When students have finished, discuss as a whole group. Key understandings for the read aloud are outlined in Box 2.1.

## Box 2.1: *Animalogies: Animal Analogies*, Key Understandings

❏ *What does a cow ALWAYS have?*
  - A cow always has hooves; the rest only some cows have.
❏ *What does a dog ALWAYS have?*
  - A dog always has a mouth; the other things the dog may have.
❏ *Look at the groups of words. Write a label for each group on the line.*
  - Dairy products
  - Bodies of water
  - Body parts
  - Shapes

# Handout 2.2: Read Aloud Reflection
*Animal Analogies* by Marianne Collins Berkes

| What does a cow ALWAYS HAVE? | What does a dog ALWAYS HAVE? |
|---|---|
| barn | collar |
| milk | mouth |
| a brand | toys |
| hooves | dog bed |

Look at the groups of words.
Write the label for each group on the line.

_____
milk
yogurt
cheese
cottage cheese

_____
river
ocean
creek
pond

_____
hand
foot
stomach
head

_____
triangle
circle
square
rhombus

# ANALYTICAL THINKING for Advanced Learners, Grades 3–5

*Skill Development Activity*

*Teacher's note*:

- ❏ Prepare the *Types of Analogies* Mini-Book (Handout 2.3) for each student.
    - ■ Print each page single sided.
    - ■ Fold the front/back cover in half. The crease should be on the left side of the front cover.
    - ■ Fold each of the inner pages in half with the text facing outward. The crease should be on the right side of the even-numbered pages.
    - ■ Stack folded book pages so that even page numbers are stacked sequentially facing the top, starting with page 2.
    - ■ Place the stack of folded interior pages inside of the folded cover page. Loose edges should be against the cover's fold, with the creased edge of the internal pages facing outward.
    - ■ Staple along the left-hand side, using the provided staple lines as a guide.
    - ■ If desired, place a strip of tape along the left-hand side to cover the staples, trimming any excess.
- ❏ Distribute the *Types of Analogies* Mini-Book to each student. Guide students through reading about the different types of analogies and completing the examples. Allow students to keep this resource to use throughout this section. Possible solutions can be found in Box 2.2.

## Box 2.2: Types of Analogies Examples

- ❏ *Examining Similarities*: Rabbits and rats are similar because they are both mammals and rodents.
- ❏ *Same Group Analogies*: A dog and a cat are both animals. A spoon and a fork are both utensils. Robin is to blue jay as pine is to oak.
- ❏ *Synonym Analogies*: Two is to double as stream is to brook, narrow is to skinny as buy is to purchase.
- ❏ *Antonym Analogies*: Poor is to rich as short is to tall, low is to high as hurry is to slow.
- ❏ *Part to Whole Analogies*: A pillow is a part of a bed, and a cushion is a part of a chair.

**Handout 2.3** Types of Analogies Mini-Book

Name: _____

# Types of Analogies

A comparison of two things to show their similarities or relationships.

:  :

:  :

:  :

This : this :: that : that

This **is to** this **as** that **is to** that

# What is an ANALOGY?

An analogy is a comparison between two things. It is a statement in which one pair of words share a relationship to another pair of terms.

They are written in this format:

open : close :: up : down

Which is read:

open **is to** close **as** up **is to** down

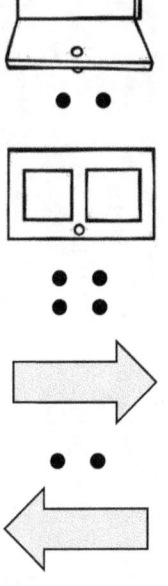

# EXAMINING SIMILARITIES

When creating analogies, you must recognize similarities in order to categorize words or ideas.

For example,

 and  are similar because they both look happy.

## YOUR TURN

How are these pictures alike?

Rabbits and rats are similar because...

# Same Group ANALOGIES

Same group analogies focus on how two things are similar. The first pair of words names two things in a certain group. The second pair must also follow this pattern.

**How are ___ and ___ related?**

Dog is to cat as spoon is to fork

How is the first pair related? _____

How is the second pair related? _____

**YOUR TURN**

robin : blue jay :: pine : _____

---

# Synonym ANALOGIES

Words that have almost the same meaning are called synonyms. This type of analogy uses two pairs of words that have similar meanings.

**What word means the same as ___?**

Chuckle is to laugh as slice is to cut

The first pair of words are synonyms, and the second pair are synonyms.

**YOUR TURN**

two : double :: stream : _____

narrow : skinny :: buy : _____

# Antonym ANALOGIES

Words that have the opposite meaning are called antonyms. This type of analogy uses two pairs of words that have opposite meanings.

**What word means the opposite of _____?**

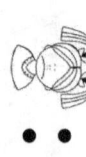

sad is to happy as mend is to cut

The first pair of words are antonyms and the second pair are antonyms.

## YOUR TURN

poor : rich :: short : _____

low : high :: hurry : _____

# Part to Whole ANALOGIES

fin is to fish as wing is to bat

A fin is a part of a fish, and a wing is a part of a bat.

**What is _____ a part of?**

This type of analogy focuses on parts of other things. For example, a page is a part of a notebook.

## YOUR TURN

pillow : bed :: cushion : chair.

A _____ is a part of _____ and a _____ is a part of _____.

# Object/Function ANALOGIES

This type of analogy focuses on how the objects are used.

**What does a ____ do?**

broom : sweep :: hammer : hit

broom is to sweep as hammer is to hit.
Think how are the objects used?

**YOUR TURN**

pencil : write :: scissors : ____

chair : ____ :: ladder : ____

# Cause & Effect ANALOGIES

This type of analogy focuses on the cause-and-effect relationship between words.

**What causes ____ to happen?**

Hungry : eat :: thirsty : drink

Hungry is to eat as thirsty is to drink.
The cause is being hungry, and the effect is to eat.
The cause is being thirsty and, the effect is to drink.

**YOUR TURN**

trash : pollution :: hurricane : ____

tired : ____ :: ____ : itchy

# Characteristic ANALOGIES

This type of analogy focuses on the descriptions of the items.

**How would you describe _____?**

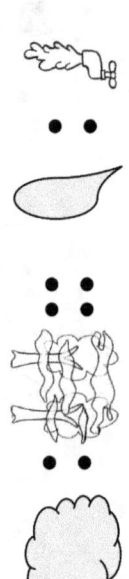

water is to liquid as fog is to gas

Think: What describes the first item in each pair?

### YOUR TURN

dog : furry :: fish : _____

candy : _____ :: jalapeno : _____

# Mathematical ANALOGIES

This type of analogy requires you to look at the mathematical relationships and use mathematical vocabulary.

**How does this concept relate to _____?**

1 :  :: 2 :

One is to one smiley face as two is to two smiley faces.

50 + 2 : 52 :: 20 + 2 : 22

Fifty plus two is to fifty-two as twenty plus two is to twenty-two.

### YOUR TURN

Triangle is to  as square is to _____

2, 4, 6, _____, 10 : 8 :: 3, 6, 9, _____, 15 : _____

- *Object/Function Analogies*: A pencil is to write as scissors are to cut, chair is to sit as ladder is to climb.
- *Cause and Effect Analogies*: Trash is to pollution as hurricane is to destruction, tired is to sleep as itchy is to scratch.
- *Characteristic Analogies*: Dog is to furry as fish is to scaley, candy is to sweet as jalapeno is to spicy.
- *Mathematical Analogies*: 2, 4, 6, __, 10 is to **8** as 3, 6, 9, __, 15 is to **12**.

---

- Distribute Completing Analogies (Handout 2.4). Direct students to carefully consider the relationships between the terms and then record their idea to complete each analogy. If this is challenging, allow students to partner while completing. Solutions for this handout can be found in Box 2.3.
- If students understand the concept, challenge them to create one more of each type of analogy.

## Box 2.3: Completing Analogies Examples

- Synonyms: 1. angry, 2. three, 3. try, 4. easy
- Antonyms: 1. right/stay, 2. whisper, 3. frown, 4. under
- Characteristics: 1. cricket/spider, 2. fish/reptile, 3. silk
- Part/Whole: 1. bear, 2. branch, 3. book
- Object/Function: 1. shovel, 2. bake, 3. heat
- Same Group: 1. banana, 2. cat, 3. pen
- Cause and Effect: 1. burn, 2. wet, 3. fall

### Optional Enrichment Activity

- Duplicate the "I Have, Who Has?" card pages (Handout 2.5), copying front-to-back, and cut apart the cards. Be sure that you have matching card fronts and backs; each card is marked with a letter (A through R) to help make sure that fronts and backs match. In this game, each

# Handout 2.4: Complete the Analogies

Name: _____

Fill in the blank to make an analogy.

## Synonym Analogies

1. huge : enormous :: mad : _____.

2. infant : baby :: trio : _____.

3. grab : seize :: attempt : _____.

4. garbage : trash :: simple : _____.

## Antonym Analogies

1. happy : sad :: left : _____.

2. safe : dangerous :: yell : _____.

3. sleepy : awake :: smile : _____.

4. over : under :: top : _____.

## Characteristics

1. green : grasshopper :: black : _____

2. feathers : bird :: scales : _____

3. rough : sandpaper :: smooth : _____

Now you try: _____ : _____ :: _____ : _____

# Handout 2.4, continued... Complete the Analogies

Name: _____

Draw a line to the word to form the analogy.

### Part/Whole Analogies

1. stinger : bee :: claw :     branch

2. foot : yard :: leaf:        book

3. card : deck :: page :       bear

### Object/Function Analogies

1. knife : cut :: dig :        bake

2. jet : fly :: oven :         shovel

3. elevator : lift :: furnace : heat

### Same Group

1. kitchen : bedroom :: apple :   pen

2. doll : ball :: dog :           banana

3. mop : broom :: pencil :        cat

### Cause and Effect Analogies

1. stroke : swim :: fire :     wet

2. tired : yawning :: rain:    burn

3. plant : grow :: trip :      fall

# Handout 2.5: I Have, Who Has?

**A**

simple : easy :: finish :

**Who Has...**

What completes my analogy?

**B**

last : first :: joy :

**Who Has...**

What completes my analogy?

**C**

broom : sweep :: brush :

**Who Has...**

What completes my analogy?

**D**

teacher : teach :: chef :

**Who Has...**

What completes my analogy?

**E**

sit : chair :: lay :

**Who Has...**

What completes my analogy?

**F**

wood : solid :: juice :

**Who Has...**

What completes my analogy?

**Handout 2.5, continued:** I Have, Who Has?

A
I Have…
WRITE

B
I Have…
MUG

C
I Have…
DIFFERENT

D
I Have…
TRAMPOLINE

E
I Have…
SICK

F
I Have…
HUNGRY

# Handout 2.5, continued: I Have, Who Has?

**G**

true : correct :: wealthy :

**Who Has...**

What completes my analogy?

**H**

kind : cruel :: lie :

**Who Has...**

What completes my analogy?

**I**

scissors : cut :: pen :

**Who Has...**

What completes my analogy?

**J**

Police : help :: doctor :

**Who Has...**

What completes my analogy?

**K**

run : track :: jump :

**Who Has...**

What completes my analogy?

**L**

fuzzy : socks :: soft :

**Who Has...**

What completes my analogy?

**Handout 2.5, continued:** I Have, Who Has?

G
I Have...
# BED

H
I Have...
# SAD

I
I Have...
# LIQUID

J
I Have...
# COMB

K
I Have...
# PRESENT

L
I Have...
# END

**Handout 2.5, continued:** I Have, Who Has?

**M**

afraid : scared :: gift :

**Who Has...**

What completes my analogy?

**N**

stone : rock :: ill :

**Who Has...**

What completes my analogy?

**O**

eraser : pencil :: handle :

**Who Has...**

What completes my analogy?

**P**

lost : found :: same :

**Who Has...**

What completes my analogy?

**Q**

drink : thirsty :: eat :

**Who Has...**

What completes my analogy?

**R**

beak : bird :: snout :

**Who Has...**

What completes my analogy?

**Handout 2.5, continued:** I Have, Who Has?

| M  I Have…  PIG | N  I Have…  BLANKET |
|---|---|
| O  I Have…  COOK | P  I Have…  RICH |
| Q  I Have…  TRUTH | R  I Have…  HEAL |

# ANALYTICAL THINKING for Advanced Learners, Grades 3–5

student will be given a card with part of an analogy on one side and an answer to an analogy on the other. (Differentiation: allow students who might need more support to be paired with other students). There are 18 cards; some students may have to work in pairs, or some may take more than one card depending on your numbers; all cards should be used.

❏ Starting with any student, ask them to read their analogy fill in the blank and "Who Has" question. For example, "I have 'simple is to easy as finish is to ____.' Who has the answer to my analogy?" Students should look at their analogy answers (the "I Have" side) and see who has an answer that makes the most sense to complete the analogy. They should provide reasoning for their answers. (Ex.: "I have *end*. I know that's the answer because *simple* and *easy* are synonyms and so are *finish* and *end*.")

❏ The student who had that analogy answer will then turn over their card and read their scenario and "Who Has" analogy question.

❏ The game continues in this manner until all cards have been read and analogies have been made.

❏ Discuss: What clues did we use to make analogies? Were some cards trickier than others? Why? Reiterate that we needed to make the same connection between each set of terms to complete accurate analogies.

## Asking Questions Lesson 2: Writing Questions about the World

**Objective:** Understand the difference between thick and thin questions.

### Materials

❏ Device to display panda image
  - https://www.si.edu/object/giant-panda:nzp_NZP-20050824-264JC
❏ Handout 2.6: Thin Anchor Chart (one enlarged copy for the class)
❏ Handout 2.7: Thick Anchor Chart (one enlarged copy for the class)
❏ Handout 2.8: Thick or Thin Question Sort (one per partner pair)
❏ *Why?* by Lindsay Camp and Tony Ross (teacher's copy)
❏ Handout 2.9: Read Aloud Reflection (one per student)
❏ Handout 2.10: Asking Questions about Nature (one per student)
❏ Magnification tools, such as magnifying glasses

## Whole Group Introduction

*Teacher's note*: Before showing students the giant panda image from the Smithsonian, click on the expand button. Once the image is expanded, there is a + sign to zoom in. Zoom in so just the upper left ear of the panda is in focus.

- ❏ Remind students that asking good questions is a skill they can develop.
- ❏ Display the zoomed in image. Tell students they are going to play 20 Questions by observing the image and asking yes or no questions to figure out what this is a picture of.
    - ■ If students are unable to guess the correct answer after 20 Questions, show students the complete image. Have students explain which questions were helpful and which questions led them astray.
    - ■ If students guess the correct answer, ask students to explain how their observations and questioning helped them come to the right conclusion.
- ❏ Explain that there are different types of questions. Some questions are thin and require just a one-word answer, like the yes or no questions they asked in the 20 Questions game. Other questions are thick, requiring more thought and having longer explanations.
- ❏ Display the anchor charts for Thick (Handout 2.7) and Thin (Handout 2.6) Questions. Explain the difference between the two types of questions. Allow students to generate a few thick and thin questions with a partner about the panda image.
- ❏ Distribute the Thick or Thin Question sort (Handout 2.8). Allow partners to cut and sort the questions as either thick or thin. Discuss as a whole group and then allow students to glue the sort on a sheet of paper.

## Read Aloud Activity

- ❏ Introduce the story *Why?* by Lindsay Camp and Tony Ross. Tell students that this book illustrates a child's natural curiosity.
- ❏ Read aloud the story. Pause to discuss; why do you think she is asking so many questions? (To learn about the world around her.)
- ❏ Distribute the Read Aloud Reflection (Handout 2.9). Allow students to complete the top half of the paper independently or with a partner.
- ❏ Complete the bottom questions together as they are more abstract. The teacher will pose the question, allowing students to turn and talk to their neighbor about the question. Then the teacher can ask for volunteers to share their ideas. Once the ideas have been shared, decide on a synthesizing sentence for each question. Key understandings for the Read Aloud Reflection are outlined in Box 2.4.

**Handout 2.6:** Thin Questions Anchor Chart

# THIN QUESTIONS

Can be answered easily and usually with a one-word answer.

Questions start with:
Who?
What?
When?
Where?

Who is the main character?
What is her job?
When did the story take place?
Where did the story take place?

**Handout 2.7: THICK** Questions Anchor Chart

# THICK QUESTIONS

Address large, universal concepts and are harder to answer. They are open-ended and may have multiple answers.

What if?
Why did?
What caused?
Why do you think…?
How did…?
What would happen if…?
What might…?
What caused…?

# Handout 2.8: Think vs. Thin Question Sort

Name: _____

| THICK | THIN | Explain the theory of gravity. |

| Where does the story take place? | Is an elephant a mammal? | Do all trees lose their leaves? |

| Predict what will happen next. | How many jellybeans are in this box? | What season is it? |

| How do flies walk on the ceiling? | What are the types of trees? | What are the three states of matter? |

| What is the hollow space in the bone filled with? | How are rainbows made? | How do airplanes fly? |

| Why can I see the moon during the day? | What is the main character's name? | Why is the earth round? |

# Handout 2.9: Read Aloud Reflection
*Why?* by Lindsay Camp and Tony Ross

Name: _____

Summarize the main idea of the story.

How did Lily's questions to the aliens impact the story?

## WHY ASK WHY?

What is the purpose of asking questions?

What makes a question a good one?

When is curiosity a good thing?

When is curiosity a bad thing?

# ANALYTICAL THINKING for Advanced Learners, Grades 3–5

> ### Box 2.4: *Why?* Key Understandings
>
> - *Story summary*: Lily asks the question "Why?" all the time. Her dad tries to answer her questions, but sometimes he's too tired and replies, "It just does, Lily." Then one day, a spaceships lands and the aliens want to destroy the earth. Lily immediately asks a series of "Why?" questions, and the aliens realize they don't have a good reason to destroy earth. So, they leave, and the earth is saved.
> - *How did Lily's questions to the aliens impact the story?*
>     - The aliens realized they didn't have a good reason to destroy the planet and decided to leave.
> - *What is the purpose of asking questions?*
>     - It is important to ask questions to learn about the world.
> - *What makes a question a good one?*
>     - Good questions are open-ended and allow for serious contemplation.
> - *When is curiosity a good thing?*
>     - Curiosity can be good when you are learning about the world. Asking questions to understand things is a good thing.
> - *When is curiosity a bad thing?*
>     - Perhaps, when you are being curious about something that doesn't involve you, such as gossip.

## Skill Development Activity

- Tell students they are going to be making observations about their world and generating questions.
- In this lesson, students will be examining something from nature closely and asking questions. You may choose to:
    - Take students on a nature walk around the playground. Tell students they are to choose one item from nature to bring back to the classroom. Suggest things like a rock, shell, leaf, flower, twig, or grass.
    - Hand out objects you have already collected from outside.
- Distribute Asking Questions about Nature (Handout 2.10). Once students have their nature item, tell students to draw the item using just the naked eye.

# Handout 2.10 Asking Questions about Nature

Name: _____

Observing my _____

Observation with the naked eye.

Observation using a magnifying glass.

Write 2-3 **THICK** questions about your item.

- ❏ Then distribute either magnifying glasses or jeweler's loupes. Tell students to carefully observe the intricate parts of their item and draw a close-up view.
- ❏ After drawing their item, tell students to write two or three questions about their item. Remind students that analytical thinkers ask deep questions that may begin with "I wonder, why, how, or what might…"

## Asking Questions Authentic Application Activity: Writing Nature Similes

**Objective:** Ask questions to determine relationships between ideas/objects.

### Materials

- ❏ *Quick as a Cricket* by Audrey Wood (teacher's copy)
- ❏ Handout 2.11: Writing Nature Similes (one per student)
- ❏ One small pine tree branch for demonstration, or an internet-curated image of one

### Read Aloud Activity

- ❏ Introduce the story *Quick as a Cricket* to the students. Tell students that this book uses similes to describe the boy. Tell students similes compare two unlike things using *like* or *as*. For example, this story compares the boy and the cricket's speed. *The boy is as quick as a cricket.* As you read, pause to discuss how the author is comparing the boy to animals.

### Skill Development Activity

- ❏ Remind students of the nature observations they completed in the previous lesson. Tell students they will now be writing nature similes based on the item they have selected.
- ❏ Explain that using the following question stems, they can compare their item to another object and create similes.
- ❏ Model completing the Writing Nature Similes (Handout 2.11) with a pine tree branch. See below for examples.

# Handout 2.11 Writing Nature Similes

Name: _____

| What other items does my _____ | |
|---|---|
| look like? | because they both: |
| sound like? | because they both: |
| feel like? | because they both: |
| smell like? | because they both: |

Write a simile for each sense.

My _____ is

as _____ as a _____.

as _____ as a _____.

as _____ as a _____.

as _____ as a _____.

## Pre-Writing Nature Similes

| What other items does my pine tree branch... | |
|---|---|
| **look like?** A bumpy frog | **because they are both** green |
| **smell like?** A flower | **because they are both** fragrant |
| **sound like?** A mouse | **because they are both** quiet |
| **feel like?** Porcupine | **because they are both** prickly |

- ❏ Model how to turn the ideas from the chart into similes.
  - ■ My pine branch is as green as a frog.
  - ■ My pine branch is as fragrant as a flower.
  - ■ My pine branch is as quiet as a mouse.
  - ■ My pine branch is as prickly as a porcupine.
- ❏ Distribute Writing Nature Similes (Handout 2.11). Guide students to use their Observation and Questioning about Nature (Handout 2.10) to help complete this chart.
- ❏ Encourage students to interact with their natural object from the previous lesson again, using all of their senses to observe.
- ❏ Students will use their senses to make connections and answer the following questions:
  - ■ What item does my item look like? Because they both...
  - ■ What item does my item smell like? Because they both...
  - ■ What item does my item sound like? Because they both...
  - ■ What item does my item feel like? Because they both...
- ❏ After completing the chart, students should collaborate with a partner to make sure their explanations make sense.
- ❏ Finally, students will write their nature similes on the bottom half of the page. If time permits, allow students to share their smiles with the group.

## Asking Questions Concluding Activities

- ❏ Distribute the Asking Questions Exit Ticket (Appendix A). Ask students to reflect on their learning about the skill of generating thick questions to learn about the world. Allow time for students to complete the exit ticket. Use this as a formative assessment to gain a better understanding of your students' readiness to effectively practice the skill of questioning.
- ❏ If desired, complete the Group Asking Questions Rubric (Appendix A) to track students' progress with the skill.

❏ If desired, use the Analytical Thinking Student Observation Rubric (Appendix A) to assess and quantify individual students' mastery.
❏ Ask students to retrieve their Analytical Thinking Avatar (Handout I.4). In the Asking Questions box, they should either write the main ideas of this section or illustrate their avatar using the skill of asking questions.

## Bibliography

Berkes, M. (2011). *Animalogy: Animal analogies.* Mount Pleasant, SC. Arbordale Publishing.

Camp, L. and Ross, T. (1998). *Why?* New York: Putnam.

Cohen, J. (August 24, 2005). *Giant Panda.* Washington, DC: Smithsonian's National Zoo & Conservation Biology Institute. https://www.si.edu/object/giant-panda:nzp_NZP-20050824-264JC

Pixar. (October 30, 2019). Pixar Forky asks a question – official trailer [video]. *YouTube.* https://www.youtube.com/watch?v=4e4UKAOgk_k&list=PLc-UfGbMhhShgWau-Zd4Un1TmNa29jSuQ&index=2

Wood, A. (1982). *Quick as a cricket.* New York: Child's Play.

# CHAPTER 3

# Sub-Skill 3
## *Classifying and Organizing*

**TABLE 3.1**
Classifying and Organizing Sub-Skill Overview

| | Thinking Skill Outline |
|---|---|
| **Focus Questions** | ❏ How can we think about this?<br>❏ What do we wonder? |
| **Lesson 1** | *Sorting into Sets*<br>❏ **Trade Book Focus:** *Sort It Out!* by Barbara Mariconda<br>❏ **Practice Activity:** Sets |
| **Lesson 2** | *Belonging to Sub-Sets*<br>❏ **Trade Book Focus:** *I Am Josephine (and I Am a Living Thing)* by Jan Thornhill and Jacqui Lee<br>❏ **Practice Activity:** Sub-Sets |
| **Authentic Application Activity** | *Venn Diagrams and Dichotomous Keys*<br>❏ **Practice Activity:** Students will complete a dichotomous key and Venn diagrams while learning about animal classifications. |

# ANALYTICAL THINKING for Advanced Learners, Grades 3–5

## Classifying and Organizing
## Lesson 1: Sorting into Sets

**Objective:** Sort and group items by rules.

### Materials

- Handout 3.1: Classify and Organize Anchor Chart (one enlarged copy for the class)
- Handout 3.2: Classify and Organize Open Sort (one per student)
- *Sort It Out!* by Barbara Mariconda (teacher's copy)
- Handout 3.3 Read Aloud Reflection (one per student)
- Attribute Blocks (optional)
- Handout 3.4: Classifying and Organizing Sets (one per student)
- Handout 3.5: Creating Sets (one per student)

### Whole Group Introduction

- Ask students: What is classifying? What is organizing? Are they always synonymous? If students do not have any background knowledge, just proceed to the introduction.
- Introduce the Classify and Organize Anchor Chart (Handout 3.1), pointing out how these skills require students to group information in a meaningful way and determine the "rules" for the grouping. Explain that organizing is the act of sorting, while classifying is the act of creating the "rules" of the sort.
- Distribute the Introducing Classifying and Organizing Sets page (Handout 3.2). Instruct students to cut out each item and do a free sort (students choose how to sort the pictures), grouping the items.
- Ask students to share how they sorted the pictures.
- Tell students they need to re-sort their picture cards in a completely different way. Challenge students to sort the cards over and over, noting how the "rules" for categorizing change each time.

### Read Aloud Activity

- Show the cover of the book *Sort It Out!* to the students. Tell students this mouse has a collection of items which he will organize and

**Handout 3.1:** Classify & Organize Anchor Chart

# CLASSIFY & ORGANIZE

## GROUPING INFORMATION IN A MEANINGFUL WAY

# Handout 3.2 Introducing Classifying and Organizing: SETS

Name: _____

categorize. Ask if any of the students have collections and if they have sorted their collections in any specific ways. If students have personal examples, allow one or two to share systems that have worked for them.
- ❏ Read the story aloud, pausing at various points to discuss ways to organize and classify the items.
- ❏ After reading, explain that the mouse sorted his items by looking at their attributes. Remind students that an attribute is a characteristic shared by the items in the group.
- ❏ Distribute the Read Aloud Reflection page (Handout 3.3).
- ❏ Direct students to carefully consider and answer the questions. When students have finished, discuss as a whole group. Key understandings for the read aloud can be found in Box 3.1.

## Box 3.1: *Sort It Out!* Key Understandings

- ❏ Packy must sort through his huge collection of trinkets and put them away.
- ❏ Packy sorted his items into groups based on their characteristics and attributes.
- ❏ What do these have in common?
  - ■ Types of dogs
  - ■ Types of air transportation
  - ■ Types of body parts
  - ■ Types of utensils
  - ■ Types of liquids
  - ■ Types of clothing

### Skill Development Activity

- ❏ Introduce the concept of sets. A set is a collection or group of things that are alike in at least one way. Show the Classify and Organize Anchor Chart (Handout 3.1). Ask students: How is each ring a set? The shapes inside each ring are the same.
- ❏ If students are struggling with the concepts of sets, remind them of the sorting they did with the attribute blocks. You may wish to model grouping sets of blocks based on certain attributes. For example, put a hula hoop on the ground and put all circles in the hoop. Ask students

# Handout 3.3: Read Aloud Reflection
*Sort it Out!* by Barbara Marioconda

Name: _____

| Summarize the main idea of the story. | How did the book show classifying and organizing? |
|---|---|
|  |  |

## What do they have in common?

1. Beagle, Pug, dalmatian, and mutt are all _____.

2. Jet, blimp, kite, plane are all _____.

3. Legs, stomach, eyes, lungs are all _____.

4. Fork, spoon, knife, chopsticks are all _____.

5. Soda, juice, milk, blood are all _____.

6. Shoe, jacket, shirt, skirt are all _____.

what is the rule for this set? Continue modeling this until students understand the concept.
❏ Distribute Classifying and Organizing Sets (Handout 3.4). Allow students to work independently or with a partner to complete. Circulate to correct anyone who is off-track. Solutions for Handout 3.4 can be found in Box 3.2.

## Box 3.2: Classifying and Organizing Sets Answer Key

❏ In the circle: 15, 29, 77, 19, 109, and 99.
❏ All the animals in this set *can fly*.
❏ All the animals in this set *are insects*.
❏ The members of this set all have *dots and stripes*.

❏ Distribute Creating Sets (Handout 3.5). Tell students they are going to create two sets for a friend to solve. Give students the instructions one step at a time.
  ■ First, decide upon a rule but don't write it on the paper.
  ■ Draw or write five items inside the circle which belong to the set.
  ■ Finally, put three items outside of the circle which do not fit the rule.
❏ After students have completed both circles, allow students to switch papers with a partner. See if the partner can figure out the "rules" for each set.

## Classifying and Organizing Lesson 2: Belonging to Sub-Sets

**Objective:** Classify and organize items into multiple sets and sub-sets.

### Materials

❏ *I Am Josephine (and I Am a Living Thing)* by Jan Thornhill and Jacqui Lee (teacher's copy)
❏ Handout 3.6: Read Aloud Reflection (one per student)
❏ Handout 3.7: Classifying and Organizing Sub-Sets (one per student)
❏ Handout 3.8: Creating Sub-Sets (duplicate as needed, one per student completing the enrichment activity)

# Handout 3.4 Classifying & Organizing Sets

Name: _____

Look at the letters inside and outside the circle. You will see that the letters that belong to the set are **vowels**.

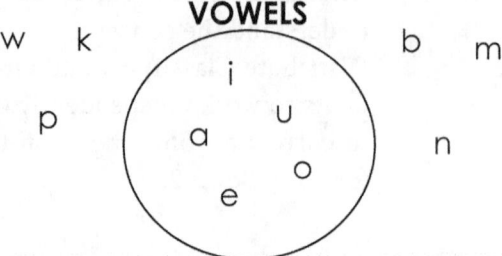

1. Write all the odd numbers inside the circle. The even numbers should go outside of the circle.

   12    77    109
   15    38    99
   29    19    86

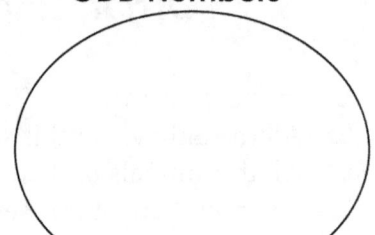

All the animals in this set
_____

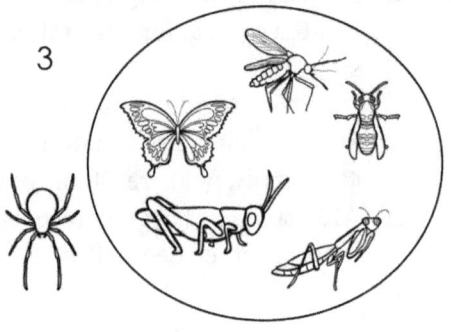

All the animals in this set
_____

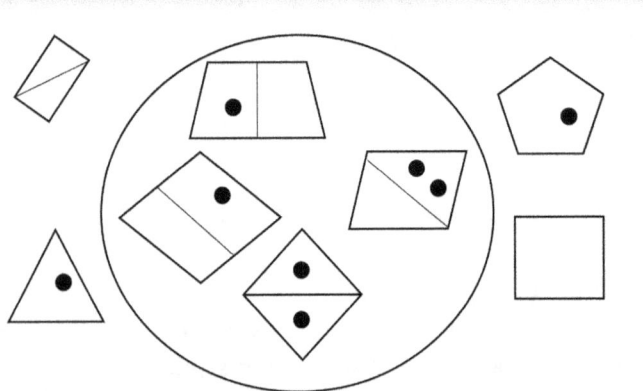

The members of this set ALL have

_____

AND

_____

**Handout 3.5:** Creating Sets

Name: _____

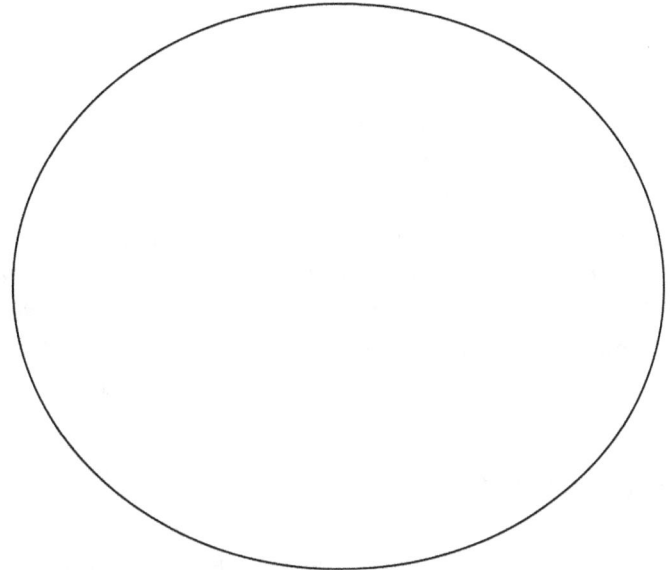

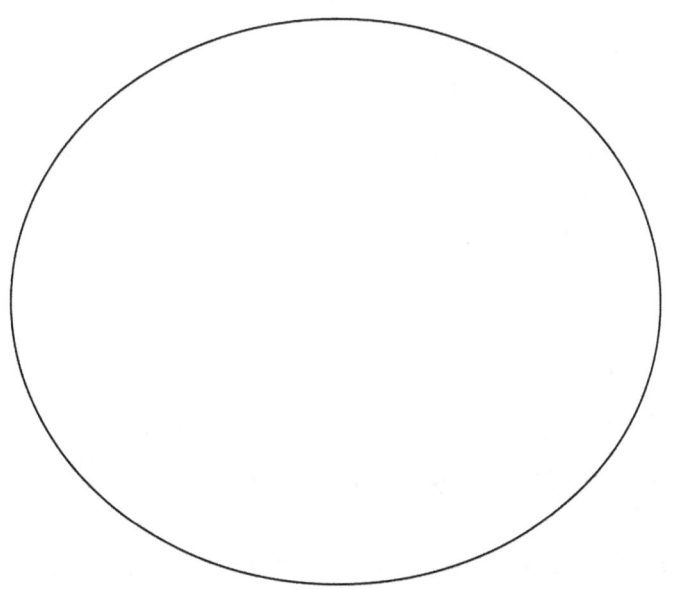

## Whole Group Introduction

- Introduce the concept of sub-sets by doing a class sort.
  - First make a circle of students in your class. Tell them that the outside ring is the set of students in our class.
  - Next, have all the girls take a step inside the circle. Explain that the girls are a **sub-set** of our class. They belong to the sub-set of the girls' circle and the set of students in this class set.
  - Direct the girls to step back to the outside circle. Next have the boys step in. Ask students to name the labels of the set and sub-set.
- Continue playing the game until most students understand the concept (options: hair color, eye color, kids who play basketball...).

## Read Aloud Activity

- Introduce the *story I Am Josephine (and I Am a Living Thing)* by Jan Thornhill and Jacqui Lee. This story will show students how we are each a part of many sets and sub-sets.
- As you read, pause to discuss what each classification means. A human being is a person. Mammals are animals who give birth to live young, have fur, and are warm-blooded. Animals are living things that have a mother and father, eat other living things, digest food, and move around. A living thing is alive, is made of cells, eats, drinks, and gets rid of waste.
- Distribute the Read Aloud Reflection (Handout 3.6). The top two sections of this page will be familiar to the students. The bottom half shows the sub-sets referenced in the story. You may need to model how to complete this diagram. Key understandings are outlined in Box 3.3.

### Box 3.3: *I Am Josephine (and I Am a Living Thing)* Key Understandings

- *Story Summary*: Josephine explores the idea that she is human being, mammal, animal, and living thing all based off the characteristics of each category.
- *Connection to Classifying and Organizing*: Josephine describes each category and explains how she is a part of each set.

# Handout 3.6: Read Aloud Reflection
*I am Josephine* by Jan Thornhill & Jacqui Lee

Name: _____

| Summarize the main idea of the story. | How did the book show classifying and organizing? |

Josephine is a member of many sets and subsets.
Add one more example to each section of the diagram.

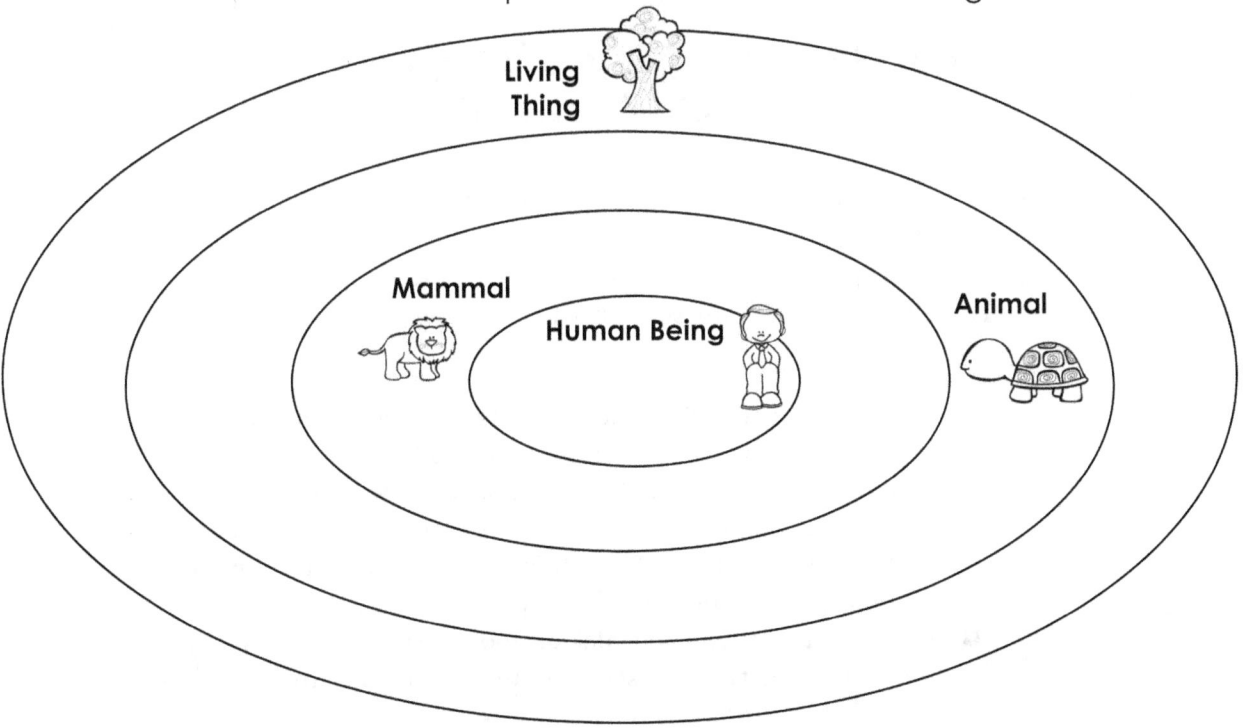

# ANALYTICAL THINKING for Advanced Learners, Grades 3–5

> ❏ *Add one more example to each section on the diagram.*
>   - Living thing: plant, organism
>   - Animal: fish, bird, reptile, amphibian
>   - Mammal: dog, cat, horse
>   - Human being: any person of their choosing

## *Skill Development Activity*

❏ Review the concept of sub-sets. Distribute Classify and Organize Sub-Sets (Handout 3.7). Tell students to carefully observe Set A and Set B. Ask students the following questions:
  - What numbers are in Set A?
  - What numbers are in Set B?
  - Which set has more numbers?
  - How do you know?

❏ Allow students who understand the concept to complete the page independently. Others may benefit from working with a partner or in a small group led by the teacher. Solutions for this handout can be found in Box 3.4.

> ## Box 3.4: Classifying and Organizing Sub-Sets Answer Key
>
> ❏ Set C is the set of <u>four-sided shapes</u>. Set D is the set of <u>trapezoids</u>. Therefore, set _D_ is a sub-set of Set _C_.
> ❏ Set F is 10, 12, 14, 16, 18, and 20; set E is 11, 13, 15, 17, and 19. Therefore, set **F** is a sub-set of set **E**.

❏ Optional Enrichment: Distribute Creating Sub-Sets (Handout 3.8) Tell students they are going to create sub-sets for a friend to solve. You may wish to provide students with scratch paper to work on their rough drafts, and once they know their rules will work, they can transfer their final set data to Handout 3.8. As this concept is abstract, we recommend giving the directions slowly, step by step.
  - First, on the scratch paper, decide upon the two rules for your sub-sets. Label the two sub-sets. Circulate to make sure the sub-set rules that students are creating will work.

# Handout 3.7 Classifying & Organizing Subsets

Name: _____

A set inside a larger set is called a **subset**.

**Set A** is all the numbers between 1 & 10
**Set B** is all the odd numbers between 1 & 10.
Therefore, Set B is a **subset** of Set A.

*HINT: Always begin with the smallest set, then work outwards.*

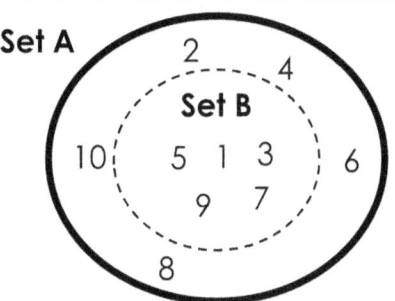

---

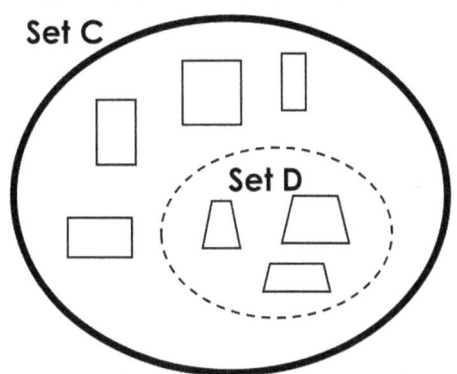

**Set C** is the set of _____

**Set D** is the set of _____

Therefore, Set ___ is a **subset** of Set ___.

*HINT: Always begin with the smallest set, then work outwards.*

---

Write the numbers in the correct set.

**Set E** is all the numbers between 10 & 20.
**Set F** is all the even numbers between 10 & 20.

Therefore, Set ___ is a **subset** of Set ___.

*HINT: Always begin with the smallest set, then work outwards*

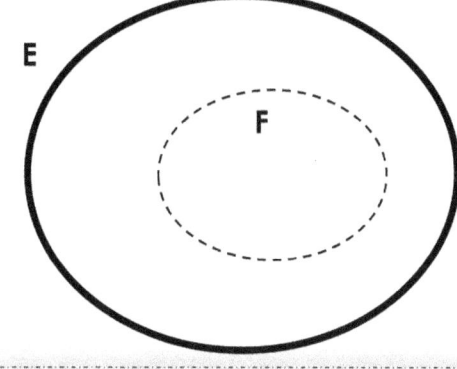

---

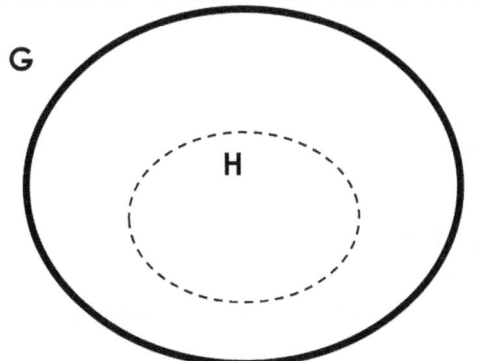

Draw at least 2 things in each set.

**Set G** is circles with dots.
**Set H** is circles with squiggles and dots.

Set ___ is a **subset** of Set ___.

*HINT: Always begin with the smallest set, then work outwards*

# Handout 3.8: Creating Subsets

Creator: _____

Create your own Subset puzzle for a friend to solve.

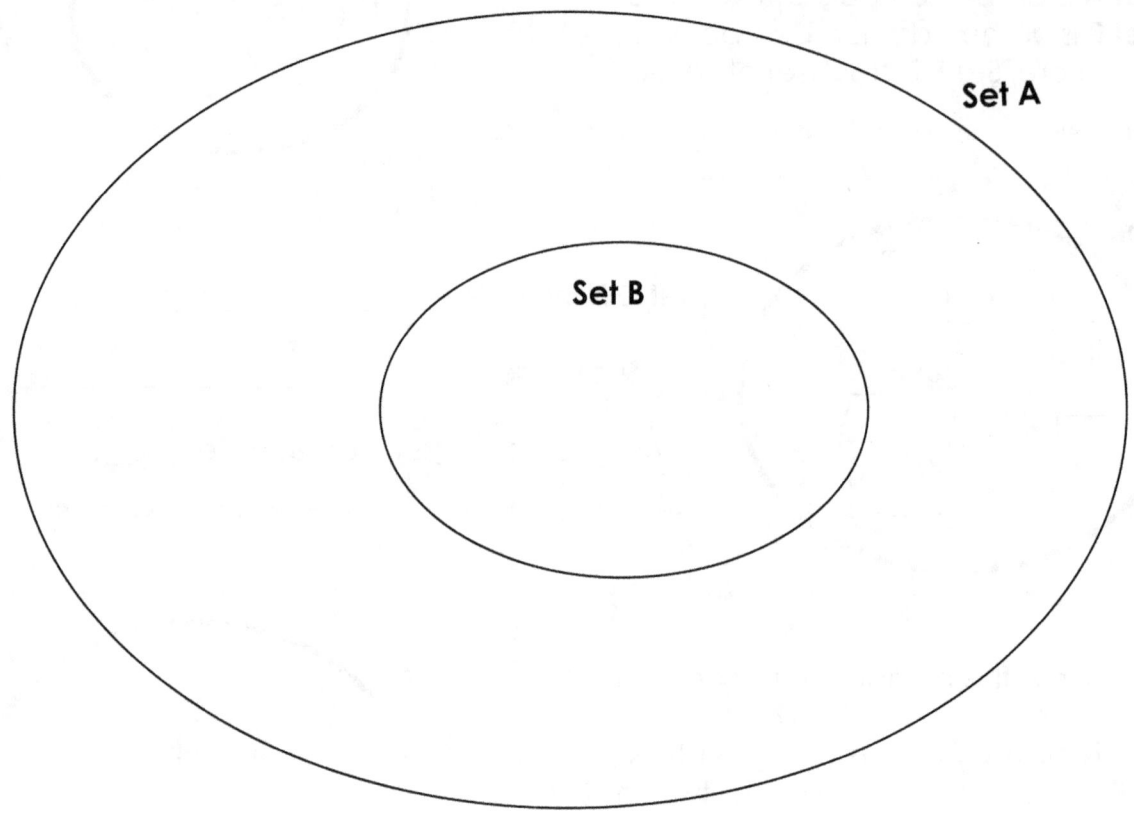

Puzzle Solver: _____

**Set A** is the set of things that _____

**Set B** is the set of things that _____

Therefore, Set _____ is a **subset** of Set _____.

HINT: Always begin with the smallest set, then work outwards.

- Next, direct students to start with the inner circle. Record between three and five items to represent the inner rule.
- Record between three and five items to represent the outer rule. Circulate to check for understanding.
- Students will transfer their sub-set puzzles to Handout 3.8. Tell students not to write the rules for their puzzles. Their partners will complete that section.
- Switch papers with a partner and complete each other's sub-set puzzles.
- After partners have completed one another's puzzles, allow students to discuss what made this activity challenging.

## Classifying and Organizing Authentic Application Activity: Venn Diagrams and Dichotomous Keys

**Objective:** Apply the skills of classifying and organizing to animal classification.

### Materials

- ❏ Handout 3.9: Vertebrates poster (one enlarged copy for the class)
- ❏ Handout 3.10: Mammals poster (one enlarged copy for the class)
- ❏ Handout 3.11: Birds poster (one enlarged copy for the class)
- ❏ Handout 3.12: Reptiles poster (one enlarged copy for the class)
- ❏ Handout 3.13: Amphibians poster (one enlarged copy for the class)
- ❏ Handout 3.14: Fish poster (one enlarged copy for the class)
- ❏ Handout 3.15: Vertebrate Animal Classification Notes (one per student)
- ❏ Handout 3.16: Vertebrate Dichotomous Key (one per student)
- ❏ Handout 3.17: One-Set Venn diagram (one per student)
- ❏ Handout 3.18: Two-Set Venn diagram (one per student)
- ❏ Handout 3.19: Three-Set Venn diagram (duplicate as needed)
- ❏ Handout 3.20: Four-Set Venn diagram (duplicate as needed)
- ❏ Handout 3.21: Invertebrate Dichotomous Key (one per student)
- ❏ Scissors

### Whole Group Introduction

- ❏ Prior to this activity, post the five animal classification posters (Handouts 3.9, 3.10, 3.11, 3.12, 3.13, and 3.14) around the classroom,

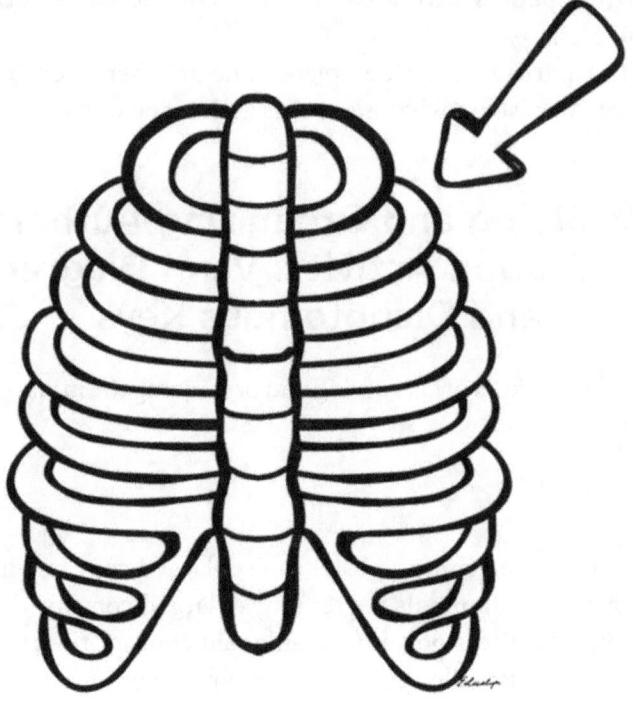

**Handout 3.10:** Mammals Anchor Chart

# MAMMALS

- HAVE BACKBONES
- HAVE HAIR ON THEIR BODIES
- ARE WARM BLOODED
- HAVE A LARGE MUSCLE CALLED A DIAPHRAGM WHICH IS USED TO BRING AIR INTO THE LUNGS.
- HAVE MAMMARY GLANDS THAT PRODUCE MILK FOR THEIR YOUNG
- ALMOST ALL GIVE LIVE BIRTH

RABBITS
BAT
DOLPHIN
LION

**DID YOU KNOW?**
Warm-blooded means their internal body temperature does not change much when the temperature outside changes.

# BIRDS

- HAVE BACKBONES
- ARE WARM-BLOODED
- HAVE FEATHERS COVERING THEIR BODIES
- HAVE WINGS FOR FLIGHT
- HAVE HOLLOW, LIGHTWEIGHT BONES TO ALLOW FOR FLYING MORE EASILY
- HAVE BEAKS AND NOT TEETH
- BREATHE WITH LUNGS
- LAY EGGS

OSTRICH
GEESE
BALD EAGLE
HERON

**DID YOU KNOW?**
Warm-blooded means their internal body temperature does not change much when the temperature outside changes.

**Handout 3.12:** Reptiles Anchor Chart

# REPTILES

- HAVE BACKBONES
- MAY LIVE ON LAND OR IN WATER
- HAVE DRY, SCALY SKIN THAT IS WATERPROOF
- ARE COLD-BLOODED ~ IF THEY ARE:
  - TOO COLD, THEY BASK IN THE SUN
  - TOO WARM THEY SEEK WATER OR SHADE
- BREATHE WITH LUNGS
- MOST LAY EGGS
- LOOK LIKE THEIR PARENTS FROM THE TIME THEY HATCH

ALLIGATORS
SNAKES
LIZARDS
TURTLES

**DID YOU KNOW?**
Cold-blooded means their internal body temperature changes when the temperature outside changes.

Handout 3.13: Amphibians Anchor Chart

# AMPHIBIANS

- HAVE A BACKBONE
- ARE COLD-BLOODED
- LIVE IN PLACES THAT ARE DAMP
- MOST LAY EGGS
- MANY ARE BORN IN WATER AND GO THROUGH CHANGES: EGGS ⇒ TADPOLES ⇒ ADULTS
- BREATHE THROUGH GILLS DURING TADPOLE STAGE
- LOSE THEIR GILLS AND TAILS AND GROW LUNGS

FROGS
TOADS
SALAMANDERS
NEWTS

**DID YOU KNOW?**
Cold-blooded means their internal body temperature changes when the temperature outside changes.

**Handout 3.14:** Fish Anchor Chart

# FISH

- HAVE BACKBONES
- ARE COLD-BLOODED
- LIVE IN WATER THEIR ENTIRE LIVES
- HAVE FINS AND TAILS FOR SWIMMING
- MOST HAVE SCALES COVERING THEIR BODIES
- BREATHE WITH GILLS INSTEAD OF LUNGS
- MOST LAY EGGS

SHARK
SEAHORSE
CATFISH
GOLDFISH

**DID YOU KNOW?**
Cold-blooded means their internal body temperature changes when the temperature outside changes.

with enough space between each for students to move freely in groups between posters.
- ❏ Tell students that scientists classify animals into two main groups. Ask students if they know the names of the two groups and if they can explain the difference. If no one can name the groups, tell students:
  1. Vertebrates are animals with a backbone.
  2. Invertebrates are animals without backbones.
- ❏ Tell students they will be learning about the different classes (groups) of vertebrates today by going on a gallery walk. Distribute Vertebrate Animal Classification Notes (Handout 3.15). Divide the class into five groups. Each group will begin at a different animal classification.
- ❏ Students will have 3–5 minutes per animal classification to record facts onto Handout 3.15 before rotating to the next poster in the gallery walk.
- ❏ Students will take their animal notes (Handout 3.15) back to their desks. The notes may be used to complete the next activities.
- ❏ Distribute Dichotomous Key Chart (Handout 3.16). Tell students to cut out the animals at the bottom. They will be classifying the animals using a **dichotomous key**. This is a set of choices involving two statements that lead to the name or classification of the animal.
- ❏ Model asking the first question: Tell students to pick up the fox card. Does the animal have fur? The answer is yes, so then put the animal that has fur in the "yes" box and label it "mammal." Tell students to move the rest of the animal cards to the "no" side.
- ❏ Continue asking the "yes/no" questions, putting the correct animal in each box, labeling the animal class, and sliding the additional animals to the "no" side. Continue until all animals are correctly placed, glued, and labeled. Solutions for the dichotomous key can be found in Figure 3.1.

## Skill Development Activity

- ❏ Tell students that another way to compare animal classes is to use the idea of sets.
- ❏ Model how to record information on a one-circle Venn diagram. Explain that the overarching category is "vertebrates" and within that group we will be focusing on the sub-set of "mammals." In this Venn diagram, all the true statements about mammals go in the circle. Ask students to provide the facts that should go inside the Venn diagram (see Figure 3.2).

# Handout 3.15 Vertebrates Animal Classification Notes

Name: _____

## MAMMALS

## BIRDS

## REPTILES

## AMPHIBIANS

## FISH

# Handout 3.16 Dichotomous Key 1

Name: _____

**Vertebrates**

- Does it have fur?
  - yes → ☐
  - no → Does it have feathers?
    - yes → ☐
    - no → Does it have dry skin?
      - yes → ☐
      - no → Does it have scales?
        - yes → ☐
        - no → ☐

# Sub-Skill 3

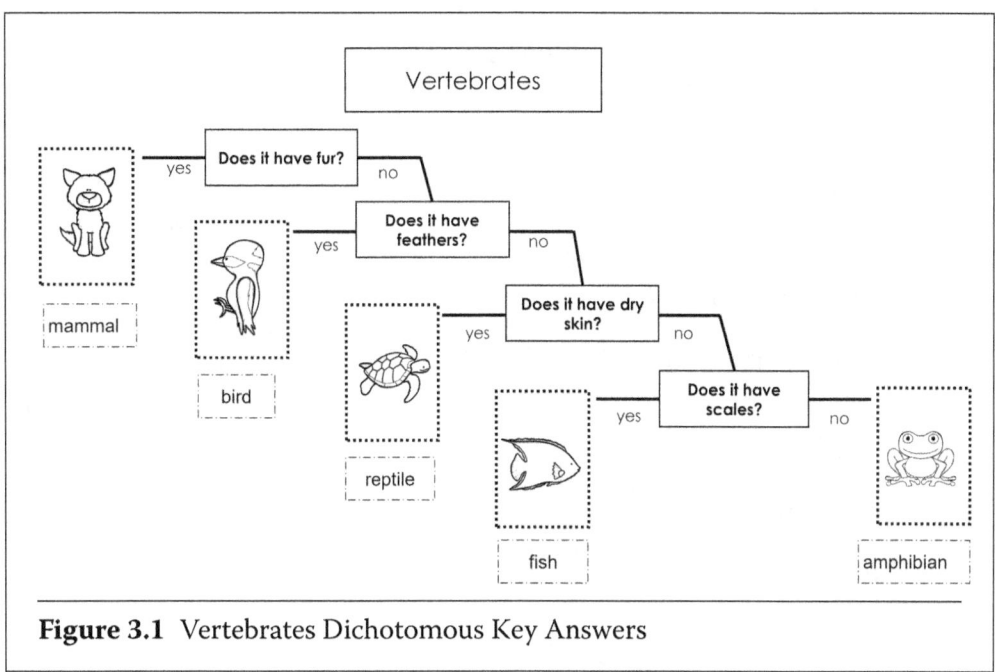

Figure 3.1  Vertebrates Dichotomous Key Answers

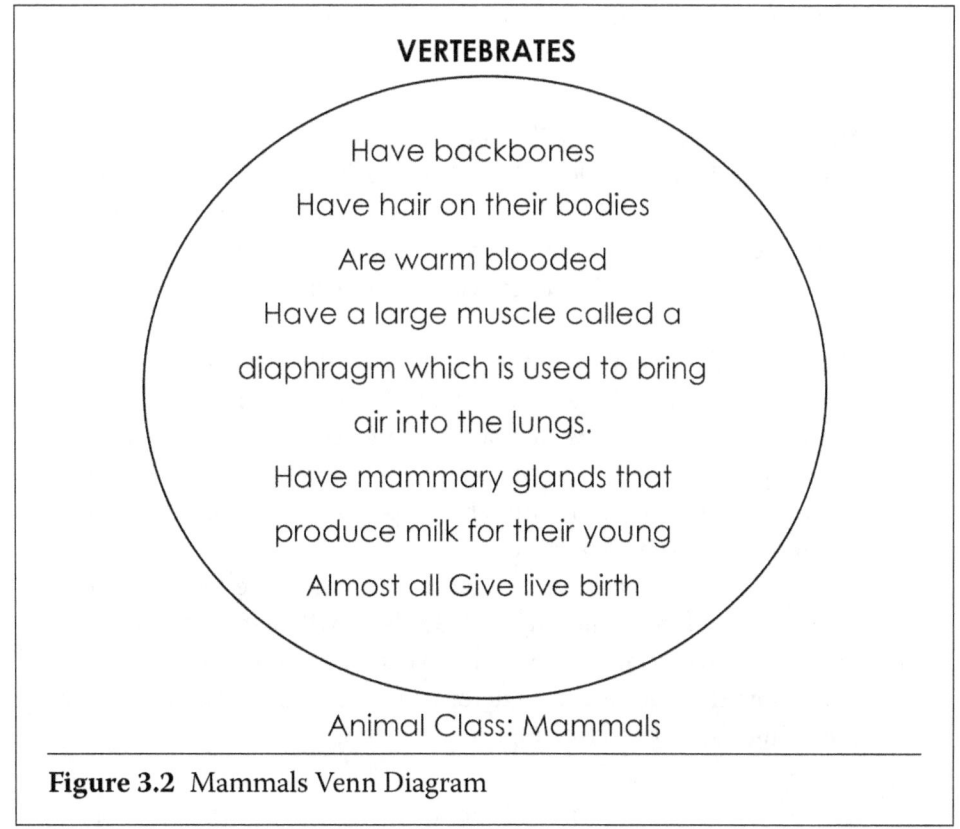

Figure 3.2  Mammals Venn Diagram

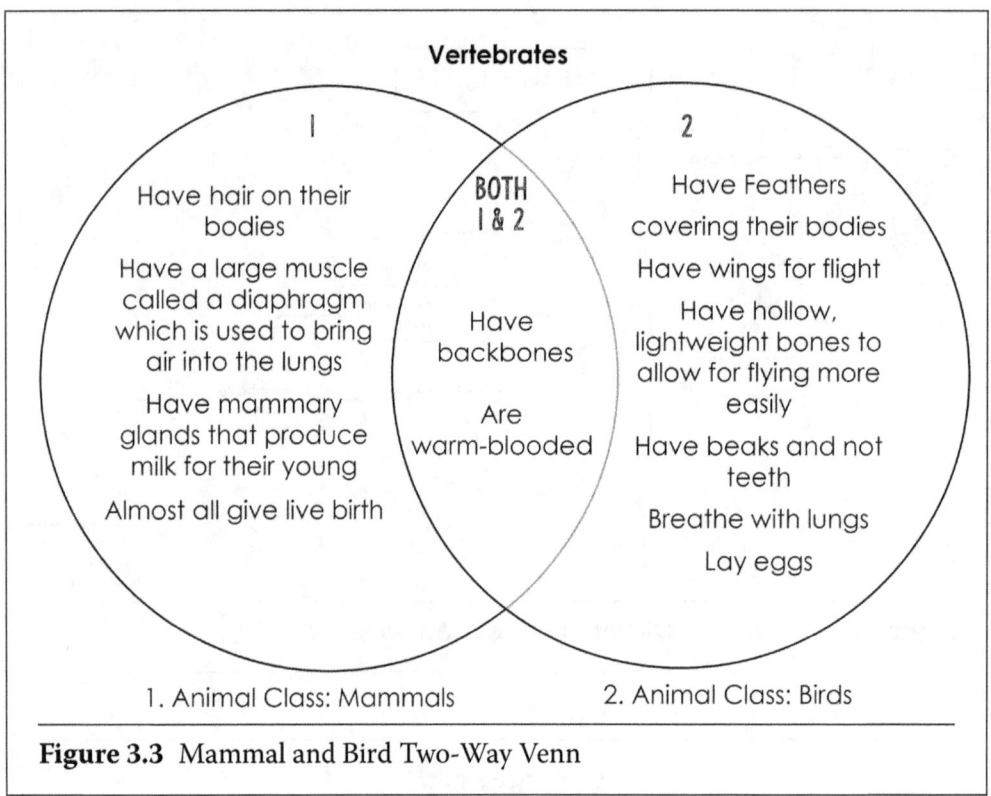

**Figure 3.3** Mammal and Bird Two-Way Venn

- ❑ Next, tell students they will now be comparing two animals. Explain that the circles are labeled with a 1 for just mammal information, 2 for bird information, or Both 1 and 2 for facts they share. Ask students to provide the facts and to name the category that the fact should go in. Model recording the characteristics in the correct area of the Venn (see Figure 3.3).
- ❑ Students will now complete their own Venn diagram comparing animal classifications. There are four levels of Venn diagrams in this activity; as the number of circles increases, the level of complexity increases. This requires students to compare more classes, which is much more abstract. Choose, or allow students to choose, the level of Venn circles based on interest and readiness.
- ❑ To conclude this chapter, students will complete the Invertebrate Dichotomous Key (Handout 3.21). Students will learn a different variation of the Dichotomous Key. In this version, they will select the animal and follow the statements to determine the invertebrate classification the animal belongs to (see Figure 3.4).

### Invertebrate Dichotomous Key

|   | Common Name | Invertebrate Classification |
|---|---|---|
| A | worm | annelid |
| B | sea sponge | porifera |
| C | starfish | echinoderm |
| D | spider | arthropod |
| E | clam | mollusks |
| F | jellyfish | cnidaria |

**Figure 3.4** Invertebrates Dichotomous Key Answers

# Handout 3.17: Classify & Organize Application: Venn 1

Name: _____

Choose 1 animal class, record the characteristics of this class in the circle.

**VERTEBRATES**

**ANIMAL CLASS:** _____

# Handout 3.18: Classify & Organize Application: Venn 2

Name: _____

Choose 2 animal classes to compare and contrast. Record the characteristics in the correct part of the Venn.

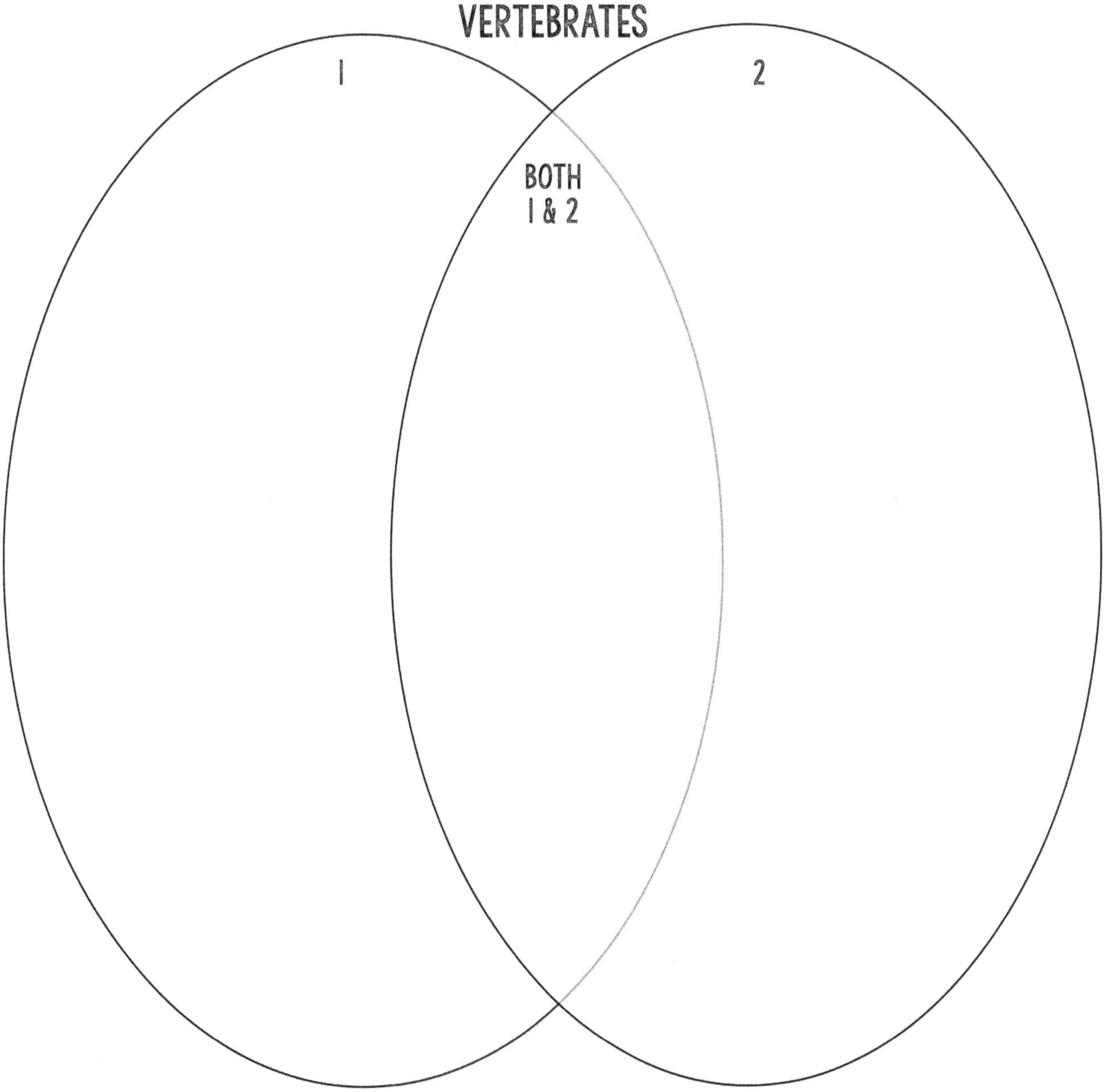

## VERTEBRATES

1

2

BOTH
1 & 2

1. ANIMAL CLASS: _____    2. ANIMAL CLASS: _____

# Handout 3.19: Classify & Organize Application: Venn 3

Name: _____

Choose 3 animal classes to compare and contrast. Record the characteristics in the correct part of the Venn.

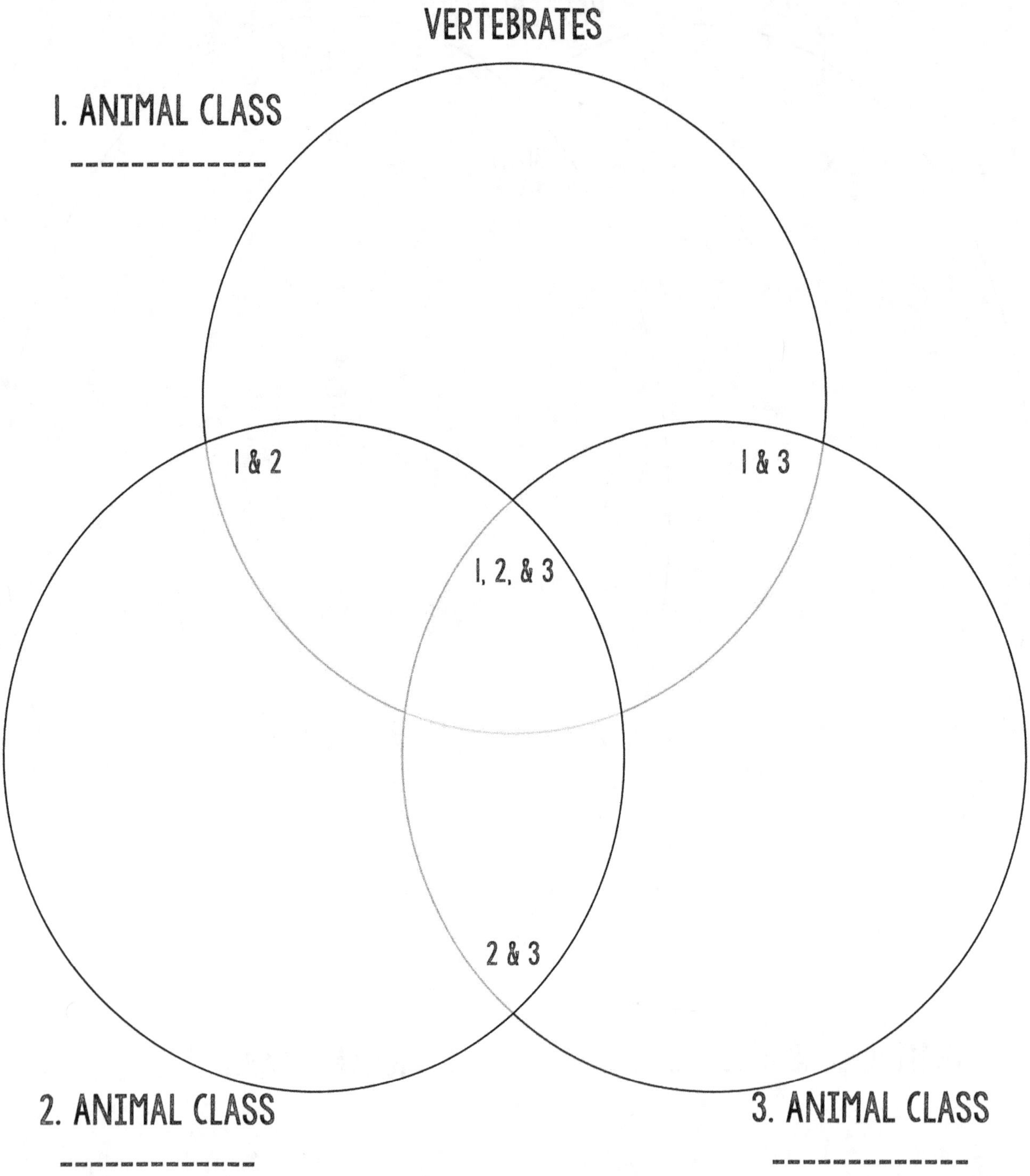

VERTEBRATES

1. ANIMAL CLASS
-------------

1 & 2

1 & 3

1, 2, & 3

2 & 3

2. ANIMAL CLASS
-------------

3. ANIMAL CLASS
-------------

# Handout 3.20: Classify & Organize Application: Venn 4

Name: _____

Choose 4 animal classes to compare and contrast. Record the characteristics in the correct part of the Venn.

## VERTEBRATES

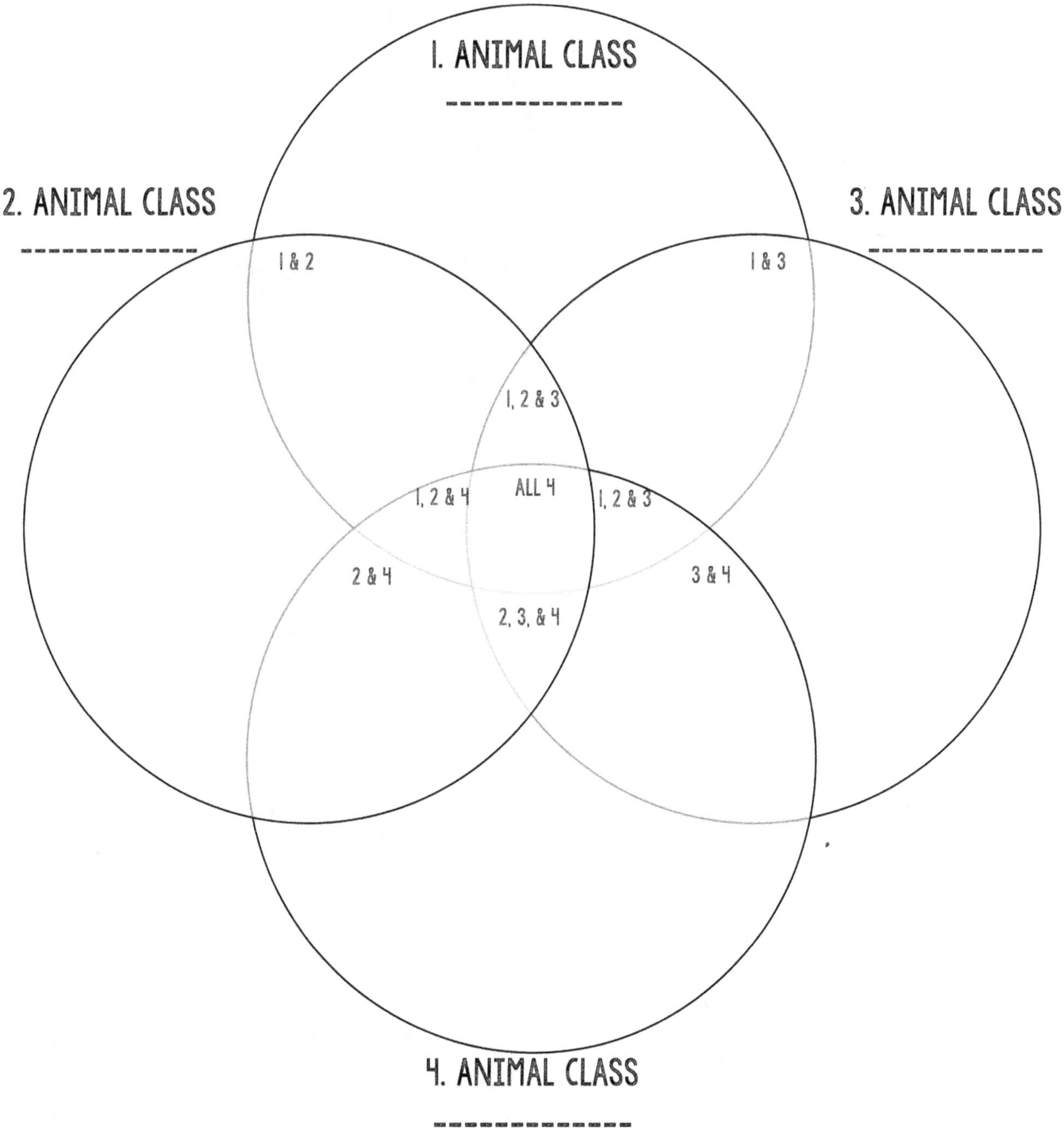

**1. ANIMAL CLASS**
-------------

**2. ANIMAL CLASS**
-------------

**3. ANIMAL CLASS**
-------------

1 & 2

1 & 3

1, 2 & 3

1, 2 & 4  ALL 4  1, 2 & 3

2 & 4

3 & 4

2, 3, & 4

**4. ANIMAL CLASS**
-------------

# Handout 3.21: Invertebrate Dichotomous Key

Name: _____

Invertebrates do not have an internal skeleton or bones. They have soft inner bodies. Some are covered with an exoskeleton or shells while others do not have any protection. Using the Dichotomous Key questions below, figure out which animal belongs to each classification.

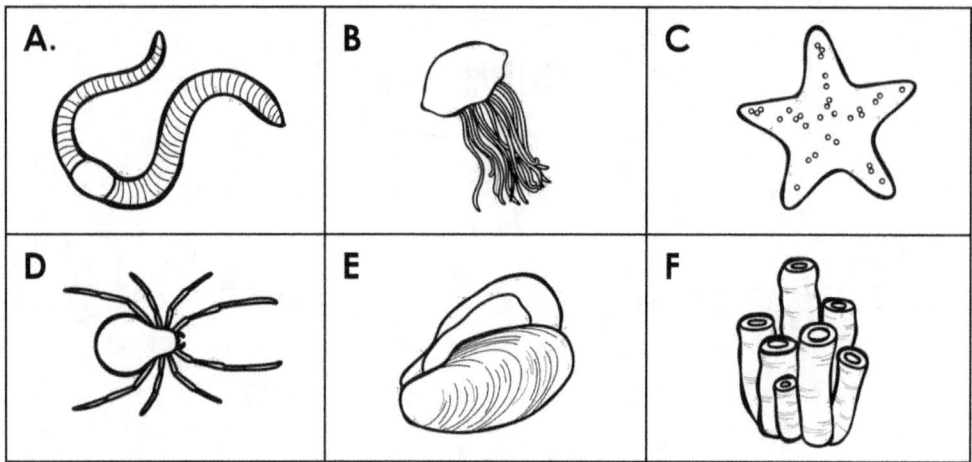

| 1 | Lives on land… Go to 2<br>Lives underwater… Go to 3 |
|---|---|
| 2 | Has legs… Go to 5<br>Does not have legs: annelid |
| 3 | Does not have a shell… Go to 4<br>Has an Internal or external shell: mollusks |
| 4 | Has a body made of a jelly-like substance: cnidaria<br>Has radial symmetry…Go to 5<br>Body acts like a water filter: porifers |
| 5 | Has jointed legs: arthropod<br>Has non-jointed leg: echinoderm |

|   | Common Name | Invertebrate Classification |
|---|---|---|
| A | worm | |
| B | sea sponge | |
| C | starfish | |
| D | spider | |
| E | clam | |
| F | jellyfish | |

## Classifying and Organizing Concluding Activities

❏ Distribute the Classify and Organize Exit Ticket (Appendix A). Ask students to reflect on their learning about the skills of grouping information in a meaningful way. Allow time for students to complete the exit ticket. Use this as a formative assessment to gain a better understanding of your students' readiness to effectively practice the skills of classifying and organizing.
❏ If desired, complete the Group Classifying and Organizing Rubric (Appendix A) to track students' progress with the skill.
❏ If desired, use the Analytical Thinking Student Observation Rubric (Appendix A) to assess and quantify individual students' mastery.
❏ Ask students to retrieve their Analytical Thinking Avatar (Handout I.4). In the Classify and Organize box, they should either write the main ideas of this section or illustrate their avatar using the skills of grouping information in a meaningful way.

## Bibliography

Bagaria, J. Set theory. In E.N. Zalta (Ed.), *The Stanford encyclopedia of philosophy* (Spring 2020 ed.). <https://plato.stanford.edu/archives/spr2020/entries/set-theory/>.

Griffing, L.R. (2011). Who invented the dichotomous key? *American Journal of Botany, 98*(12). https://doi.org/10.3732/ajb.1100188

Mariconda, B. (2008). *Sort it out!* Mount Pleasant, SC: Arbordale Publishing.

Thornhill, J. (2016). *I am Josephine (and I am a living thing)*. Berkeley, CA: Owlkids Books.

# CHAPTER 4

# Sub-Skill 4

## Make a Hypothesis

**TABLE 4.1**
Make a Hypothesis Sub-Skill Overview

| | Thinking Skill Outline |
|---|---|
| **Focus Questions** | ❑ What conclusions can we reasonably make based on this information?<br>❑ How can we test if this idea is correct?<br>❑ How can we use our observations and schema to make predictions? |
| **Lesson 1** | *Using Observations to Make a Hypothesis*<br>❑ **Trade Book Focus:** *The Thingamabob* by Il Sung Na<br>❑ **Practice Activity:** Analyzing Mathematical Patterns to Create a Hypothesis |
| **Lesson 2** | *Curiosity Breeds More Questions*<br>❑ **Trade Book Focus:** *Ada Twist, Scientist* by Andrea Beaty<br>❑ **Practice Activity:** The Four Question Scientific Strategy |
| **Authentic Application Activity** | *Introduction to the Scientific Method*<br>❑ Step 1: Ask a Question<br>❑ Step 2: Create a Hypothesis |

# ANALYTICAL THINKING for Advanced Learners, Grades 3–5

## Make a Hypothesis Lesson 1: Using Observations to Make a Hypothesis

**Objective:** Introduce the concept of making a hypothesis by using observations to make a prediction.

### Materials

- Handout 4.1: Make a Hypothesis Anchor Chart (one enlarged copy for the class)
- Handout 4.2: Read Aloud Reflection (one per student)
- Device to display the short video clip and image: "Automated Self-Operating Napkin" by Rube Goldberg
  - Video clip available at: https://www.youtube.com/watch?v=SyuukbzJvB8
  - Image available at: https://knowledgestew.com/incredible-rube-goldberg-machines
- *The Thingamabob* by Il Sung Na (teacher's copy)
- Handout 4.3: Analyzing Patterns to Create a Hypothesis (one per student)

### Whole Group Introduction

- Ask students: What is a hypothesis? Is it more than just a guess? How?
- Introduce the skills of making a hypothesis to the students. Show the Making a Hypothesis Anchor Chart (Handout 4.1). Point out how these skills require students to predict an outcome based on what they know. (At this time, you may want to delineate *hypothesis*, singular, from *hypotheses*, which is plural.)
- Tell students that a hypothesis is a statement or idea which gives an explanation to a series of observations and can be tested.
- Explain that it is often stated in an "If, then" format. A hypothesis is a prediction which can be tested and either confirmed ("yes, it's true") or refuted ("no, it's not true"). For example: If I leave my popsicle outside in the sun, then it will probably melt, because it got too warm. This is not guaranteed, but something we can test.
- Show students the Automated Self-Operating Napkin video clip. Ask students to look for cause and effect relationships. This clip is

**Handout 4.1:** Making a Hypothesis Anchor Chart

# MAKING A HYPOTHESIS

☀ + 🚰 = 🌼

## PREDICTING BASED ON WHAT WE KNOW

short so you may want to play it a couple of times for students to see each reaction.
- ❏ Project the Self-Operating Napkin Rube Goldberg machine image.
- ❏ Tell students that Rube Goldberg was a cartoonist who drew crazy inventions to do very simple tasks. The Self-Operating Napkin goes through many cause and effect relationships to wipe a man's face.
- ❏ Draw students' attention to the image. You will provide the "if" statement, and the students will try and make a "then" hypothesis as to what will happen next.
    - A. If you raise your spoon to your mouth, then (it will pull a string).
    - B. If the string is pulled, then (the ladle will move).
    - C. If the ladle is pulled back, then (it will throw a cracker in the air).
    - D. If the cracker flies up in the air, then (it will go past the bird).
    - E. If the cracker goes past the bird, then (the bird will jump off the perch to get it).
    - F. If the bird jumps off the perch, then (the perch will be knocked off balance).
    - G. If the perch is unbalanced, then (the seeds will spill into the pail).
    - H. If the seeds spill into the pail, then (the extra weight in the pail will pull a cord).
    - I. If the cord is pulled, then (it will open a box).
    - J. If the box is opened, then (a fire will light a rocket).
    - K. If the rocket is lit, then (the hook will pull a string).
    - L. If the hook pulls the string, then (the napkin will swing back and forth to wipe the man's face).
- ❏ Explain that this is a fun example of creating "If, then" statements to show cause-and-effect relationships. However, scientists create their hypotheses by wondering about the world, making observations, and then predicting an outcome based on what we know.

### Read Aloud Activity

- ❏ Introduce the story *The Thingamabob* by Il Sung Na. This story takes an elephant through a journey trying to figure out what his "thingamabob" is used for.
- ❏ Point out to the students that the elephant has many hypotheses as to what he can do with the "thingamabob." Pause periodically and ask students to tell you an "If/then" hypothesis statement from the pictures. For example, if the elephant sits in the thingamabob, then it will sail across the water.
- ❏ After reading, ask students, "How can we use our observations to make an educated guess at a solution?"

❏ Distribute the Read Aloud Reflection page (Handout 4.2). Direct students to carefully consider and answer the questions on the top half. When students have finished, discuss responses as a whole group. Then, direct students to complete the hypotheses on the bottom half of the page. Tell students to choose something that would make sense in the blank. Key understandings are outlined in Box 4.1.

> ### Box 4.1: *The Thingamabob* Key Understandings
>
> ❏ The elephant finds a "thingamabob" and tries to discover what is it used for.
> ❏ The elephant has many hypotheses and tests his theories.
>   1. If I use the "thingamabob" as a kite, then maybe I can fly with it. Test results: Not a kite.
>   2. If I use the "thingamabob" as a boat, then maybe I can sail with it. Test results: Not a boat.
>   3. If I use the "thingamabob" as a shield, then maybe I can hide behind it. Test results: Not something he can hide behind.
>   4. If I use the "thingamabob" as an umbrella, then I won't get wet. Test results: Yes, it's an umbrella.
> ❏ Writing Hypotheses
>   1. If I put ice in the sun, then *it will melt*.
>   2. *If I forget my coat*, then I will be cold at recess.
>   3. If I boil water, then *steam will rise*.
>   4. Students generate their own idea.

## Skill Development Activity

❏ Remind students that a hypothesis is a proposed explanation for a phenomenon. Hypotheses connect concepts by specifying the expected relationship between concepts and formulating a prediction of what will happen next.
❏ Tell students that both scientists and mathematicians look for patterns when creating their hypotheses. They use what is already known to produce a new idea to be tested.
❏ In math, a good hypothesis needs to be clear, precisely stated, and testable in some way.

# Handout 4.2: Read Aloud Reflection
*The Thingamabob* by Il Sung Na

Name: _____

| Summarize the main idea of the story. | How did this book show hypotheses? |
| --- | --- |
|  |  |

### Writing a Hypothesis

1. If I put ice in the sun, then _____

2. If _____, then I will be cold at recess.

3. If I boil water, then _____

4. If _____, then the plant will die.

5. If _____, then _____
_____

❏ The data from math experiments must be carefully analyzed in relation to the original hypothesis. This requires the data to be structured, prepared, and displayed in a logical format.

❏ Very often, the mathematical situation under analysis will appear to be complicated and unclear. The goal of mathematical experimentation is to impose a clear structure to the problem, gain clarity, and develop abstract "rules."

❏ Distribute Analyzing Patterns to Create a Hypothesis 1 (Handout 4.3). The concepts are quite abstract; therefore, you may need to heavily model this lesson. Some of your students may be ready to go and they can work through this independently.

❏ First, tell students to carefully analyze the number patterns. Tell students to look carefully at how the numbers increase or decrease. Ask students what they notice about the numbers. It may be helpful to write the addition or subtraction change above the numbers to make the patterns more visible.
  - 1, 3, 5... (all odd numbers, or increase by +2)
  - 1, 2, 4... (doubling pattern)
  - 10, 9, 7, 4... (subtract the next consecutive number)
  - 200, 190, 195... (−10 + 5)

❏ Tell students they will now be analyzing triangular pyramids. Have students record the triangular numbers below each pyramid. The triangular number is the total number of units (or squares) in the pyramid (see Figure 4.1).

❏ Ask students:
  - What pattern(s) do you notice? (A row is added to each pyramid, the number of squares added in the bottom row is the same as the height of the pyramid, etc. ...)
  - How can you use this pattern to write a hypothesis? (We know the pyramid is increasing by one more row than before, so we can make an educated guess.)
  - Hypothesis: If the pattern increases by adding a bottom row to each term, then the triangular number will continue to increase by the number of the term (or position in the sequence).

❏ Next, students will test their hypothesis. Have students complete the pyramid chart and label the increase (see Figure 4.2). Guide the students as follows:
  - Using this information, as students to predict how many squares will be in position 10. Students should each record their predictions.
  - How many rows will there be in position 10? (10)
  - How many squares will be in the bottom row? (10)
  - To find the 10th term you can add: $1 + 2 + 3 + 4 + 5 + 6 + 7 + 8 + 9 + 10 = 55$.

## Handout 4.3: Analyzing Patterns to Create a Hypothesis

Name: _____

*Analyzing patterns can help you create a reasonable hypothesis.* Look at the following sequences and write a description of the pattern.

- 1, 3, 5, 7, 9, 11, 13, 15 _____

- 1, 2, 4, 8, 16, 32, 64 _____

- 10, 9, 7, 4, 0 _____

- 200, 190, 195, 185, 190, 180, 185 _____

### Triangular Numbers

Below you will find the first five triangular pyramids. The sums of the units in each triangle is called the triangular number. Count the number of units and write it below the pyramid.

1st   2nd   3rd   4th   5th

Number of units  ____  ____  ____  ____  ____

What pattern(s) do you notice? _____

How can you use this pattern to create a hypothesis to test?
_____
_____

Write a hypothesis for this pattern:

If _____,

then _____.

**Handout 4.3 continued:** Analyzing Patterns to Create a Hypothesis

*After writing a hypothesis, mathematicians must test their theory.
Draw the next pyramid and record the triangular number.*

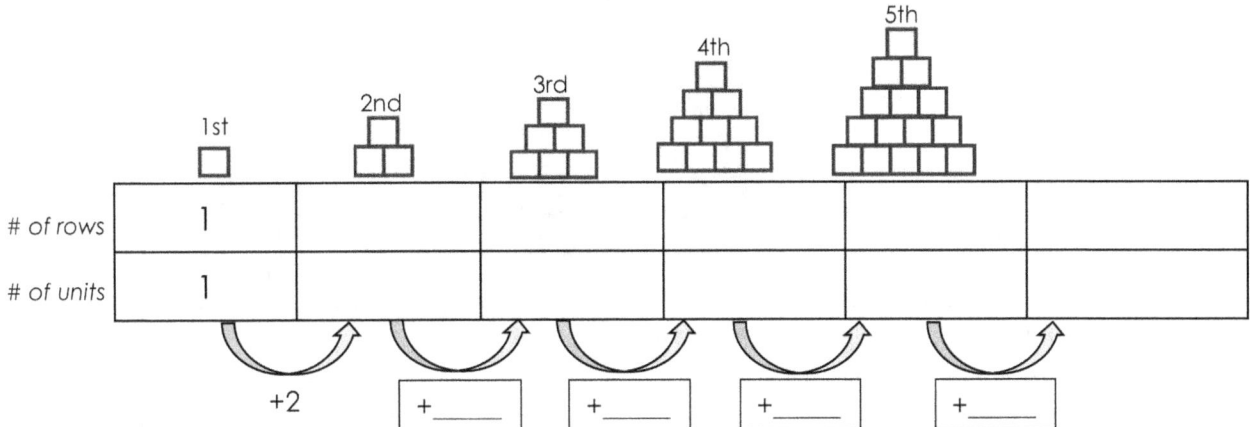

Using this information, predict how many squares will be in position 10. _____

Think, how many rows will there be in position 10? _____

How many squares will be in the bottom row? _____

So, to find the 10th term you can add: _____
_____

Try this! Match pairs of numbers like this.

1 + 10 = _____, 2 + 9 = _____, 3 + 8 = _____, 4 + 7 = _____, 5 + 6 = _____

### What pattern(s) do you notice?

- Each pair of numbers equals _____.
- There are _____ groups of _____.
- The number of pairs, _____, is half of the number of terms, _____.
- This happens because the numbers are paired in groups of _____.
- If you multiply the number of pairs _____ by the sum of each pair _____, then you will get the triangular number _____.

**CHALLENGE:** Use this pattern to figure out how many squares there would be in a pyramid with 50 rows.

# ANALYTICAL THINKING for Advanced Learners, Grades 3–5

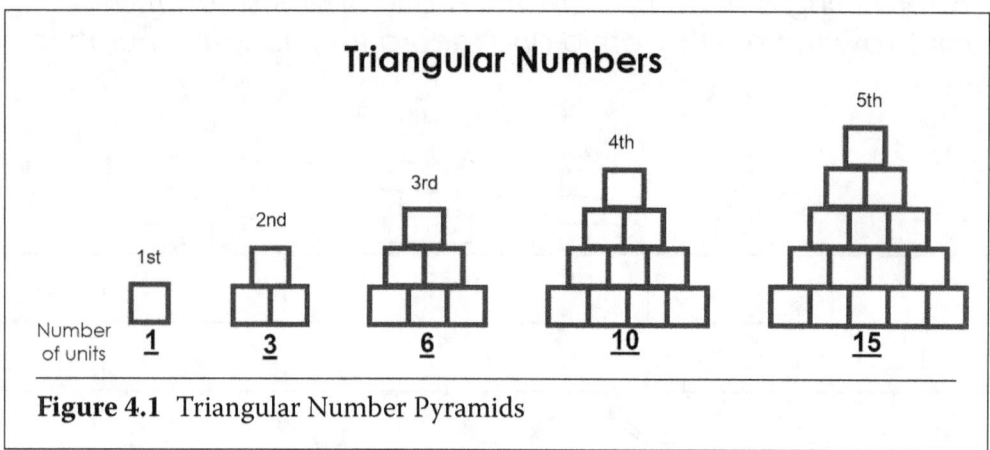

Figure 4.1 Triangular Number Pyramids

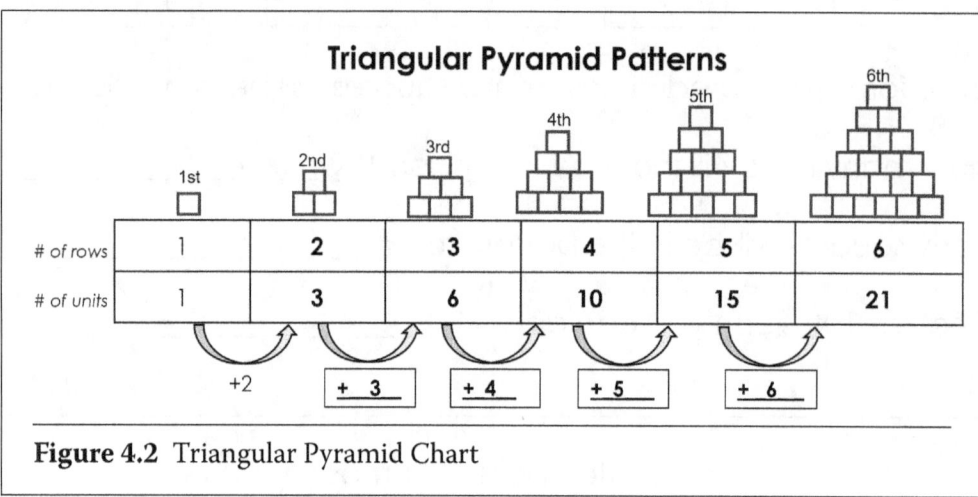

Figure 4.2 Triangular Pyramid Chart

- Show students how to match the 1st term and the 10th term (1 + 10 = 11) and then the 2nd and 9th term (2 + 9 = 11) and so on. Ask students what pattern(s) they notice.
- Each pair of numbers is equal to **11**.
- There are **5** groups of **11**.
- The number of pairs, **5**, is half of the number of terms, **10**. This happens because the numbers are paired in groups of **2**.
- If you multiply the number of pairs, **5** by the sum of each pair, **11**, then you will get the triangular number of **55**.

❏ How can you use this pattern to figure out the triangular number in the 50th position?
  - Each pair is equal to 51 (1 + 50 = 51, 2 + 49 = 51, etc. …).
  - There are 25 groups of 51.
  - 25 is half of 50, due to the numbers being paired in groups of 2.
  - If you multiply 25 by 51, the result is 1,275.

# Make a Hypothesis Lesson 2: Curiosity Breeds More Questions

**Objective:** Learn to systematically developing research experiments by starting with a hypothesis

## Materials

- *Ada Twist, Scientist* by Andrea Beaty (teacher's copy)
- Handout 4.4: Read Aloud Reflection (one per student)
- Handout 4.5: The Four Question Strategy Anchor Chart (one enlarged for the class)
- Handout 4.6: Introduction to the Four Question Strategy (one per student)
- Handout 4.7: Designing a Scientific Experiment (one per student)
- Technology to show the short video:
    - https://www.youtube.com/watch?v=D3ZB2RTylR4

## Whole Group Introduction

- Play "I'm going on a picnic." In this game, students will try to discover what items can be taken on a hypothetical picnic. The teacher will begin by saying, "I'm going on a picnic and I'm bringing… And I can go." Students will try and figure out the "rule" that must be followed to join the picnic. It can have to do with any attribute (color, shape, size, even the number of letters used to spell the name of the object). Here are some example rules:
    - Only red things can go on the picnic.
    - Only things that are spelled with five letters can go on the picnic.
    - Only things that begin with the same letter as my first name.
- Students will raise their hand to offer their guesses. "I'm going on a picnic and I'm bringing…" If the item fits the rule, say, "Yes, you can come." If it doesn't fit the rule, say, "No, I'm sorry, you can't come."
- Play a few rounds until everyone has "joined" the picnic.
- Tell students they were making hypotheses as to what the rule was to join the picnic. They had to adjust their hypothesis with the new information added each time someone was allowed to join the picnic.

# ANALYTICAL THINKING for Advanced Learners, Grades 3–5

### Read Aloud Activity

❑ Introduce the story *Ada Twist, Scientist* by Andrea Beaty. Ada Twist is a curious little girl who is constantly creating hypotheses and conducting experiments. Read the book aloud, pausing at various points asking students to identify the hypothesis.
❑ After reading, ask students: How does curiosity generate questions?
❑ Distribute the Read Aloud Reflection page (Handout 4.4). Allow students to work with a partner to answer the questions and form hypotheses. Key understandings are outlined in Box 4.2.

---

**Box 4.2: *Ada Twist, Scientist* Key Understandings**

❑ *Story summary*: Ada Twist is a curious young girl. She tries to solve a smelly mystery by generating various hypotheses and testing her theories. Ada has the heart of a scientist.
❑ *In your own words, explain what the author meant by "It's all in the head of a young scientist."*
  ■ Ada, a young scientist, observes the world, asks questions, develops hypotheses, conducts experiments, and draws conclusions.
❑ *What was Ada's first hypothesis?*
  ■ The terrible stink came from dad's cabbage stew.
❑ *What was Ada's second hypothesis?*
  ■ The terrible smell is from the cat.

---

### Skill Development Activity

❑ Tell students they will be formulating a scientific investigation using the Four Question Strategy. This strategy systematically takes the students through developing research experiments.
❑ Display the Four Question Strategy Anchor Chart (Handout 4.6). Discuss the following important ideas:
  ■ Science is the exploration of natural phenomena.

# Handout 4.4: Read Aloud Reflection
*Ada Twist, Scientist* by Andrea Beaty

Name: _____

Summarize the story in 3 sentences or less.

In your own words explain what the author meant by:

"It's all in the heart of a young scientist."

What was Ada's first hypothesis? Explain.

What was Ada's second hypothesis? Explain

What is your hypothesis?

Handout 4.5: Four Question Strategy Anchor Chart

# The Four Question Strategy

Science is the exploration of natural phenomena. Scientists wonder about the world around them. Use the Four Question Strategy to develop testable scientific questions.

### QUESTION 1
Think about what you know about a topic.
How does _____ act?

### QUESTION 2
What materials are available to conduct an experiment?

### QUESTION 3
How can I change the materials available to affect the way _____ acts?

### QUESTION 4
How can I measure or describe the response of _____ to change?

### DEVELOP INVESTIGATION QUESTIONS
- What would happen if…
- Does the amount of _____ have an affect on…

### DEVELOP A HYPOTHESIS
- Using your research experiment question, develop a hypothesis statement using the "If, then" format.

# Handout 4.6 Introduction to The Four Question Strategy

Name: _____

**Use the 4 Question Strategy to Develop Scientific Experiments.**
Think about the world around you.
What do you wonder about plants?

1. Think about what you know about plants. How do plants act?

2. What materials do we have available to conduct an experiment on plants?

3. How can I change the materials available to affect a change in the way plants act?

4. How can I measure or describe the response of the plants to the change?

- Scientists wonder about the world around them.
- Scientists ask questions to learn more about the world.

❏ Tell students, scientists often use the Four Question Strategy to design experiments about topics of interest.
  1. First, scientists think about what they already know about a topic and ask themselves: How does ____ act?
  2. Second, scientists look at the materials they have readily available to conduct an experiment on the topic.
  3. Third, scientists think about the various ways they can change the materials to affect the way the topic acts.
  4. Finally, scientists generate ways to measure or describe the response of the topic to the change.

❏ Distribute the Four Question Strategy (Handout 4.6) to each student or project one to model the process. Tell students they are going to go through the process of designing an experiment to conduct on plants; however, they will not actually be conducting this experiment. Model asking the questions and recording the students' responses. Try to prompt students to come up with multiple ideas; this is a generating session, and they will hone their ideas later. See Table 4.2 for sample responses.

❏ Distribute Designing a Scientific Controlled Experiment (Handout 4.7). Tell students they will be completing this handout using information from the video on conducting a controlled experiment. You may want the students to simply watch the video first and then debrief by completing the cloze activity on Handout 4.7 together. See Box 4.3 for a solution guide.
- Video Link: https://www.youtube.com/watch?v=D3ZB2RTylR4

## Box 4.3: Designing a Scientific Experiment Answer Guide

❏ Develop Investigation Questions:
  - What would happen if we added fertilizer to our plants?
❏ Develop a Hypothesis:
  - If we add fertilizer to our plants, then the fertilized plant will grow bigger and lusher.
❏ Develop an Experiment:
  - Pick one material to change (from Question 3); this is called the *independent variable*. We are adding *fertilizer*.

**TABLE 4.2**
The Four Questions Strategy: Plants

| 1. Think about what you know about plants. How do plants act?<br>❏ Germinate, sprout, grow, flower, die | 2. What materials do we have available to conduct an experiment on plants?<br>❏ Soil, water, seeds or small plant, light, fertilizer, containers |
|---|---|
| 3. How can I change the materials available to affect a change in the way plants act?<br>❏ Change the amount, time, or frequency of the water, fertilizer, or light | 4. How can I measure or describe the response of the plants to the change?<br>❏ Time to germinate or sprout<br>❏ Height or weight of the plant<br>❏ Leaves – number, color, size |

- The other items from Question 3 should be kept the same; this is called the *constant*. This case involves the same plant, amount of water, and light exposure. The control item is the natural condition of the item.
- One plant will be kept as a control; no *fertilizer* will be added to this plant.
- The control is what we will compare the fertilized plant to.
- Then choose what you will measure (from Question 4); this is called the *dependent variable*. We will measure the *height* of the plants.

# Make a Hypothesis Authentic Application Activity: Introduction to the Scientific Method

**Objective:** Write a scientific question and form a hypothesis.

## Materials

- ❏ Handout 4.8: Why is My Apple Brown? (one per student)
- ❏ Handout 4.9: The Four Question Strategy: Apples (one per student)
- ❏ Handout 4.10.a–f: The Scientific Method Flip Book (one per student)
  *Teacher's note*: We recommend printing the flip book from www.routledge.com/9781032199269. There you will find directions for printing and folding to make the Flip Books.

# Handout 4.7 Designing a Scientific Experiment

Name: _____

### Develop Investigation Questions

- What would happen if...
- How can we change....
- Does the amount of _____ have an affect...

Choose one question to investigate:

### Develop a Hypothesis

Using your investigation question, develop a hypothesis statement using the "If and Then" sentence format.

If _____.

Then _____.

### Develop an Experiment

- Pick one material to change (from Question 3), this is called the **independent variable.** We are adding _____.

- The other items from question 3 should be kept the same, this is called the **constant**. Same plant, amount of water, and light exposure. The control item is the natural condition of the item.
    - One plant will be kept as a control, no _____ will be added to this plant.
    - The control is what we will compare the fertilized plant to.

- Then choose what you will measure (from Question 4), this is called the **dependent variable.**
    - We will measure the _____ of the plants.

## Sub-Skill 4

### *Whole Group Introduction*

- Distribute Why is My Apple Brown? (Handout 4.8). Tell students that scientists do research before they design their experiments. Here is some background information on oxidation. Read aloud and discuss the process of oxidation. Have students write a summary of two or three sentences.
- Distribute The Four Question Strategy: Apples (Handout 4.9). Remind students that the Four Question Strategy helps scientists think about various experimental options. Once an experimental option is decided upon, the scientist will move on to utilizing the scientific method.
- Tell students that this time they will be designing and conducting an experiment on apples. Guide students through completing this process. Prompt students to generate their own ideas. Table 4.3 provides some sample responses.
- Distribute The Scientific Method Flip Book (Handout 4.10). This book will walk the students through the experimental process.
- Remind students that the scientific method provides a framework for scientists to conduct an experiment. Using the thinking from Handout 4.9, students will focus on asking a testable question and creating a hypothesis.
- The format of the flip book allows students to open to a section, read the top flap to learn about that step in the scientific method, and then record their experiment on the bottom page.
- Tell students to open their flip book to the "Ask a Question" section. Explain that scientists observe the world, wonder about the world, ask questions about the world. During this step, the students will create a testable question. Guide students through writing a question on ways to stop the apple from browning. For example: How can we change the rate at which an apple goes brown? What would happen if we put the apple in various liquids?
- Tell students to turn the page to the "Create a Hypothesis" section. Explain that scientists use prior knowledge to make an educated guess; they make predictions and form a hypothesis. A hypothesis is a statement or idea which gives an explanation to a series of observations. Guide students in writing an "If, then, because" statement. For example: If we put apple slices in milk, then they will not turn brown because the milk has vitamins and minerals. It's ok if their hypothesis is wrong. This is a great real-world lesson, as most often scientists do not generate the correct hypothesis, but disproving a hypothesis provides a lot

## Handout 4.8: Why is my Apple Brown?

Name: _____

You open you lunch box only to discover your sliced apple snack is now brown in color. What happened to the yellow flesh? This is a result of a chain of chemical reactions known as **enzymatic browning**.

During harvest time, ripe apples are picked from the tree. The skin of the apple protects it from the oxygen in the air. When the apple's skin is cut or bruised, the apple's flesh is exposed to oxygen. This begins a chemical reaction called oxidation. Oxidation causes the apple's flesh to turn brown and will eventually spoil. Oxidation makes the fruit spoil much quicker than it normally would.

Enzymatic browning is not unique to apples. Pears, bananas, and eggplants can also turn brown quickly when cut. If you prevent oxidation, you will never have to eat brown fruit again.

Explain the process of oxidation.

# Handout 4.9: The Four Question Strategy: Apples

Name: _____

1. Think about what you know about apples. How do apples act?

2. What materials do we have available to conduct an experiment?

3. How can I change the materials available to affect a change in the way apples act?

4. How can I measure or describe the response of the apples to the change?

**TABLE 4.3**
The Four Questions Strategy: Apples

| 1. Think about what you know about apples. How do apples act?<br>❏ Grow from seeds, grow on trees, good to eat, turn brown | 2. What materials do we have available to conduct an experiment on plants?<br>❏ Apples, lemon juice, milk, water, paper plates, and spoons |
|---|---|
| 3. How can I change the materials available to affect a change in the way apples act?<br>❏ Put the apple slices in various liquids | 4. How can I measure or describe the response of the apples to the change?<br>❏ Observation over a period |

of information as well. After an experiment, scientists can use what they've learned to create their next hypothesis.
❏ Tell students they will complete the experiment in the next chapter.
❏ To conclude this chapter, conduct a discussion. Ask students:
  ■ How do scientists use the skill of noticing details?
  ■ How do scientists ask questions?
  ■ How do scientists classify and/or organize the information?
  ■ How do scientists formulate a hypothesis?

## Make a Hypothesis Concluding Activities

❏ Distribute the Make a Hypothesis Exit Ticket (Appendix A). Ask students to reflect on their learning about the skill of creating a testable question and making a hypothesis statement. Allow time for students to complete the exit ticket. Use this as a formative assessment to gain a better understanding of your students' readiness to effectively practice the skill.
❏ If desired, complete the Group Asking Questions Rubric (Appendix A) to track students' progress with the skill.
❏ If desired, use the Analytical Thinking Student Observation Rubric (Appendix A) to assess and quantify individual students' mastery.
❏ Ask students to retrieve their Analytical Thinking Avatar (Handout I.4). In the "Make a Hypothesis" box, they should either write the main ideas of this section or illustrate their avatar using the skill of asking questions to create a hypothesis.

**Handout 4.10.a:** Scientific Method Flip Book

Name:

# THE SCIENTIFIC METHOD

**Handout 4.10.b:** Scientific Method Flip Book

# SCIENTISTS:
- **observe** the world around them
- **wonder** about how the world works
- **ask questions** about the world around them
- create **testable questions**

## MY RESULTS

_____
_____
_____
_____
_____
_____
_____
_____
_____
_____
_____
_____
_____

**5 · SHARE YOUR RESULTS**

**Handout 4.10.c:** Scientific Method Flip Book

## SCIENTISTS:

- **Summarize** the results in a formal written piece

- **Address your hypothesis**
  - Did the results of your experiment support your hypothesis or not?

- **Analyze your procedure**
  - Make sure to summarize the experimental procedure and comment on whether your procedure was effective in answering your scientific question.

- **Make suggestions**
  - Address potential changes that might make your experiment more effective. One common suggestion is to increase the sample size since larger samples are usually better for scientific experiments.

---

## DEVELOP A TESTABLE QUESTION:
•What would happen if…
•How can we change…
•Does the amount of _____ have an affect…

 **ASK A QUESTION**

**Handout 4.10.d:** Scientific Method Flip Book

## SCIENTISTS:
- use **prior knowledge** to make educated guesses
- make **predictions** about the world
- form a **hypothesis** which is an explanation that can be tested

## DATA: RECORD YOUR OBSERVATIONS

| Liquid | After 5 minutes | After 10 minutes | After 30 minutes |
|--------|-----------------|------------------|------------------|
|        |                 |                  |                  |
|        |                 |                  |                  |
|        |                 |                  |                  |

Based on the results of my experiment, _____
_____
_____

 **DATA COLLECTION AND ANALYSIS**

**Handout 4.10.e:** Scientific Method Flip Book

## SCIENTISTS:

- **collect and record** the data
- **analyze** the results of the experiment
- look for **cause-and-effect relationships**
- **draw conclusions**
    - If the data supports the hypothesis, conclusions may be drawn, and a recommendation made.
    - If the data does not support the hypothesis, it helps the scientist create a new hypothesis.

## DEVELOP A HYPOTHESIS:

A **hypothesis** is a statement or idea which gives an explanation to a series of observations.
It is often stated as a rule or prediction.

Using your experiment question, develop a hypothesis statement using the "If, then, because…" sentence format.

**② CREATE A HYPOTHESIS**

**Handout 4.10.f:** Scientific Method Flip Book

## SCIENTISTS:
- **Develop experiments**, which is a procedure that tests
- a hypothesis by collecting data under controlled conditions.
- Use two groups:
    1. **Control:** is the natural condition of the item
    2. **Experimental:** all the conditions are kept the same except **one condition is being tested**.
- Pick one material to change, this is called the **independent variable**
- Measure the **dependent variable** which is the response to the independent variable. It is called the **dependent** because it "depends" on the independent variable.

## DEVELOP AN EXPERIMENT

In this experiment we will test: _____

_____

The **independent variable** is _____

_____

The **dependent variable** is _____

_____

We will measure the _____

_____

### ③ CONDUCT AN EXPERIMENT

# Bibliography

Beaty, A. (2016). *Ada Twist, scientist.* New York: Abrams Books for Young Readers.

Goldberg, R. (1931). Professor Butts and the self-operating napkin. https://knowledgestew.com/incredible-rube-goldberg-machines/.

Na, I.S. (2008). *The thingamabob.* New York: Alfred A. Knopf.

Nucleus Medical Media. (April 5, 2016). Biology: Controlled experiments. *YouTube.* https://www.youtube.com/watch?v=D3ZB2RTylR4.

Sheflin, T. (October 31, 2010). The automated napkin. *YouTube.* https://www.youtube.com/watch?v=SyuukbzJvB8.

# CHAPTER 5

# Sub-Skill 5

## *Investigate and Reflect*

**TABLE 5.1**
Investigate and Reflect Sub-Skill Overview

| | Thinking Skill Outline |
|---|---|
| **Focus Questions** | ❏ How can we organize our thinking?<br>❏ Could we organize it in multiple ways? |
| **Lesson 1** | *How Does Failure Lead to Success?* |
| | ❏ **Trade Book Focus:** *11 Experiments That Failed* by Jenny Offill and Nancy Carpenter<br>❏ **Practice Activity:** Scientific Method |
| **Lesson 2** | *Analyzing Data to Determine a Conclusion* |
| | ❏ **Trade Book Focus:** *Duck & Goose* by Tad Hills<br>❏ **Practice Activity:** Draw a Conclusion and Share Results |
| **Authentic Application Activity** | *Analytical Thinking Code Breaker* |
| | ❏ **Practice Activity:** Students will use all the thinking skills learned throughout the unit to complete an Escape Game. |

# Investigate and Reflect Lesson 1: How Does Failure Lead to Success?

**Objective:** Learn to design and conduct an experiment.

## Materials

- Handout 5.1: Investigate and Reflect Anchor Chart (one enlarged copy for the class)
- Handout 5.2: Think, Think Again Puzzle 1 (one puzzle cut apart)
- *11 Experiments That Failed* by Jenny Offill and Nancy Carpenter (teacher's copy)
- Handout 5.3: Read Aloud Reflection (one per student)
- Handout 4.10: The Scientific Method Flip Book (one per student)
- Paper plates and plastic spoons (four for each group conducting the experiment)
- Apples, cut into slices of similar size (five slices per group)
- Various liquids, ½ cup per group:
  - Lemon juice
  - Vinegar
  - Water
  - Soda
  - Milk

## Whole Group Introduction

- Introduce the skills of investigating and reflecting to the students. Show the Investigate and Reflect Anchor Chart (Handout 5.1), pointing out how this requires students to examine data and draw conclusions based on the data.
- Before the lesson, cut apart the Think, Think Again Puzzle 1 (Handout 5.2). Using a document camera, display one piece of the puzzle at a time. Tell the students that it's their job to notice details and ask thoughtful questions to determine what is happening in the picture. You may want to model a noticing a small detail and asking a question.
- One by one, add each piece to the puzzle. Start with the upper left corner and then add the upper right, bottom left, bottom right, and finally the center. As you place each piece, continue asking the students:
  - What details do you notice?
  - What do you wonder?

**Handout 5.1:** Investigate and Reflect Anchor Chart

# INVESTIGATE & REFLECT

## EXAMINING DATA TO DRAW CONCLUSIONS

**Handout 5.2:** Think, Think Again: Puzzle 1

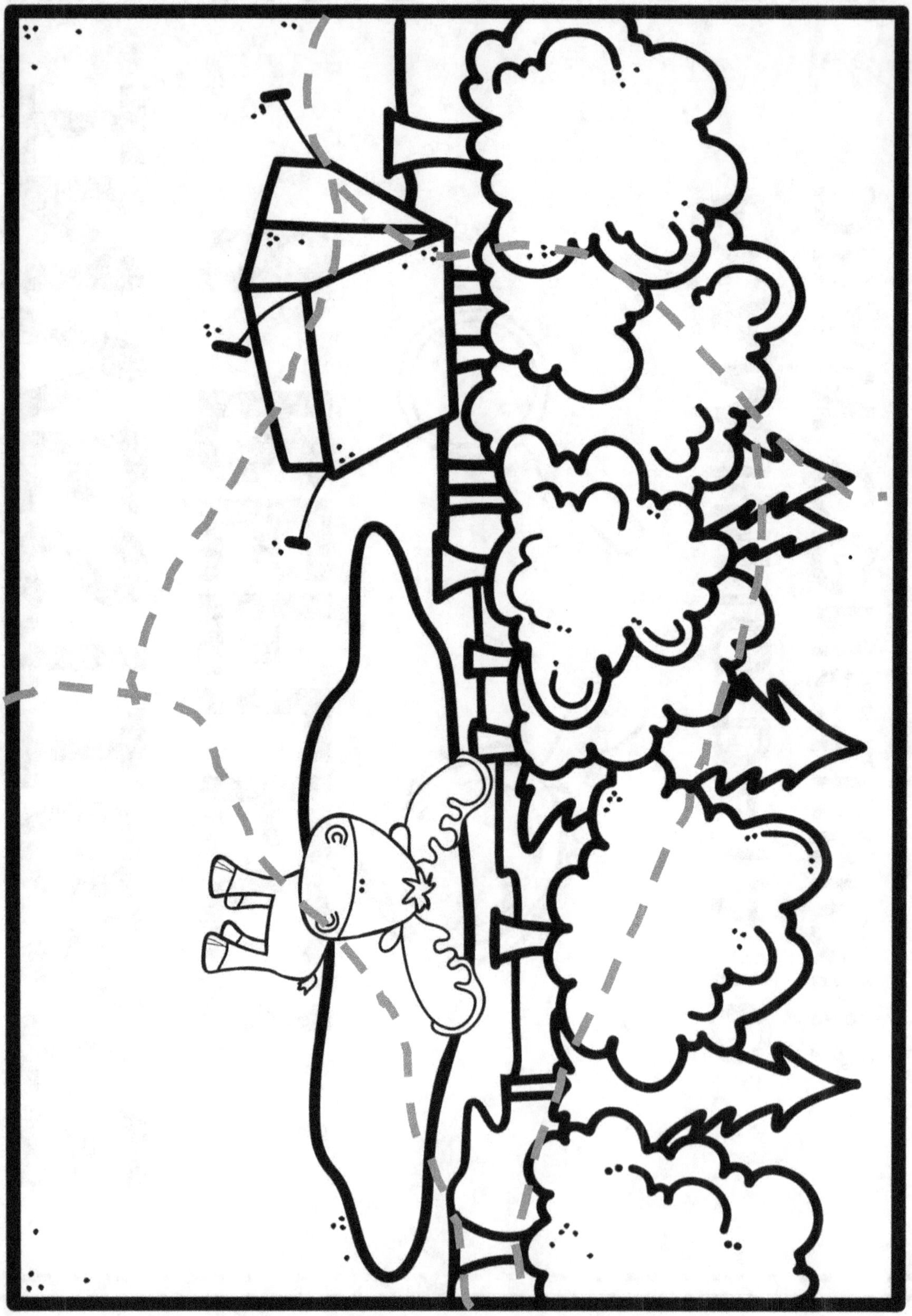

## Sub-Skill 5

- ❏ Tell students that they are being analytical thinkers by using the information known to generate questions and form hypotheses. They are *investigating* the scene and *reflecting* on the images.

### Read Aloud Activity

- ❏ Tell students that scientists must use their prior knowledge to create hypotheses and design experiments. Remind students that many scientists don't succeed in their first attempts.
- ❏ Introduce the book *11 Experiments That Failed* by Jenny Offill and Nancy Carpenter. This is a silly book which takes a budding scientist through 11 experiments. The scientist asks questions, forms a hypothesis, conducts the experiment, and reports what happened
- ❏ Distribute the Read Aloud Reflection page (Handout 5.3). Direct students to carefully consider and answer the questions on the top half. When students have finished, discuss responses as a whole group.
- ❏ Then direct students to complete the create your own silly scientific experiment. As this is an abstract activity, you may need to model it or allow students to work in pairs. Key understandings for the Read Aloud Reflection are outlined in Box 5.1.

### Box 5.1: *11 Experiments That Failed* Key Understandings

- ❏ This story takes the reader through 11 different silly scientific experiments that all go awry. Each experiment follows the scientific process: ask a question, develop a hypothesis, gather materials, conduct the experimental procedure, collect the results, and draw a conclusion.
- ❏ Create your own silly scientific experiment.
  - ■ Accept all answers which include a question, hypothesis, procedure, and conclusion.

### Skill Development Activity

- ❏ Have students take out their Scientific Method Flip Book (Handout 4.10), which they began working with in the previous sub-skill, Make a

## Handout 5.3: Read Aloud Reflection
*11 Experiments that Failed* by Jenny Offill & Nancy Carpenter

Name: _____

| Summarize the main idea of the story. | How did the book show scientific thinking? |
|---|---|
| | |

Create your own silly scientific experiment.

Question:

Hypothesis:

What you Need:

What to do:

What happened:

Hypothesis. Remind students the scientific method provides a framework to conduct experiments. Today, they will work on developing their experiment.

❏ Have students review their experimental design question and hypothesis completed in Chapter 4: Make a Hypothesis.

❏ Next, read aloud step 3: design and conduct an experiment (flip book page 3). Explain, scientists must test their hypothesis in a controlled environment. Tell students they will be testing a variety of liquids to see which liquid best preserves the apple's color and texture.

❏ Tell students, scientists must have a control group which will be an apple slice which is exposed to the air. In the experimental group, the students will be trying three to four other liquids to see which one best preserves the apple. See Box 5.2 for sample responses.

### Box 5.2: Develop an Experiment

In this experiment we will test: *How can we prevent an apple from browning so quickly?*
The independent variable is *the various liquids we will be using*.
The dependent variable is *the color of the apple slice*.
We will measure *how the apple looks after a designated time*.

❏ Split students into groups of four to conduct the experiment.
  1. Give each group four paper plates and plastic spoons.
  2. Next, teacher provides four apple slices to each group.
  3. Students observe the apples after freshly being cut.
  4. Designate and label the plates with the liquid being used. Then carefully pour a spoonful of liquid on to each apple slice.
  5. At the designated times, allow students to observe the apples and record notes.

## Investigate and Reflect Lesson 2: Analyzing Data to Determine a Conclusion

**Objective:** Reflect on the scientific process and share the results of the experiment.

## Materials

- Handout 5.4: Think, Think Again Puzzle 2 (one puzzle cut apart)
- Handout 5.5: Read Aloud Reflection (one per student)
- *Duck & Goose* by Tad Hills (teacher's copy)

## Whole Group Introduction

- Review the skills of investigating and reflecting with the students. Remind students that analytical thinkers examine the facts and data to draw conclusions based on the data.
- Before the lesson, cut apart the Think, Think Again Puzzle 2 (Handout 5.4). Using a document camera, display one piece of the puzzle at a time. Tell the students it's their job to notice details and ask thoughtful questions to determine what is happening in the picture.
- One by one, add each piece to the puzzle. Start with the upper left corner and then add the upper right, bottom left, bottom right, and finally the center. As you place each piece, continue asking the students:
  - What details do you notice?
  - What do you wonder?
- Tell students that they are being analytical thinkers by using the information known to generate questions and form hypotheses. They are investigating the scene and reflecting on the images.

## Read Aloud Activity

- Ask students what good scientists do when designing experiments. Prompt students to re-state the steps of the scientific method.
- Remind students that many scientists don't succeed in their first attempts. Introduce the book *Duck & Goose* by Tad Hills.
- After reading, ask students: How can linear thinking (thinking only according to established rules, in one singular thought pattern) lead us astray? How can we use our observations to make an educated guess at a solution?
- Distribute the Read Aloud Reflection page (Handout 5.5). Allow students to work with a partner to answer the questions. Circulate to check for understanding, targeting the key understandings outlined in Box 5.3.

# Handout 5.4: Think, Think Again: Puzzle 2

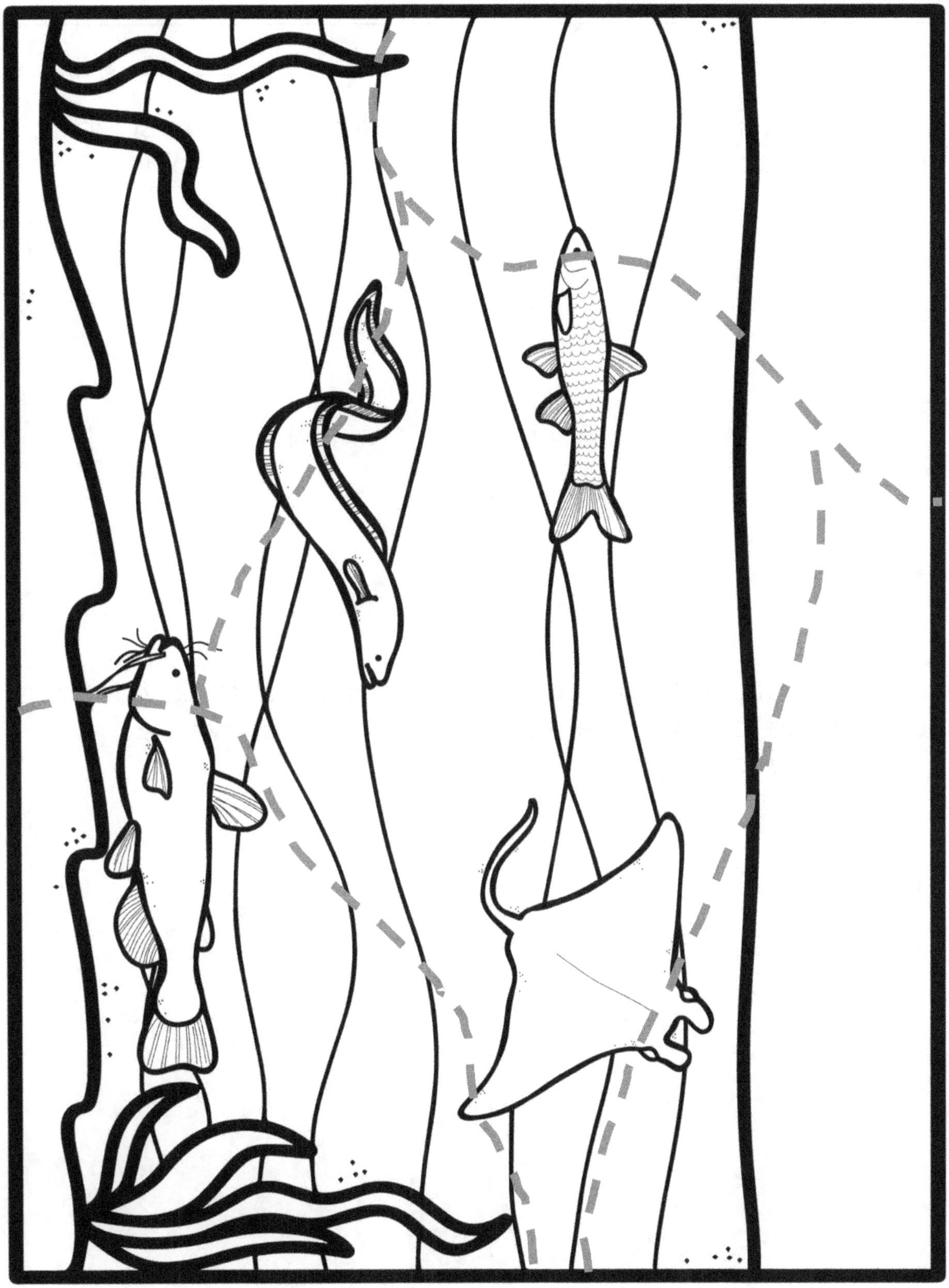

# Handout 5.5: Read Aloud Reflection
*Duck and Goose* by Tad Hills

Name: _____

| Summarize the main idea of the story. | Does the book show scientific thinking? Explain. |
|---|---|
| What observations do Duck and Goose make to determine the ball was an "egg"? | How can linear thinking lead us astray? |

## Box 5.3: *Duck & Goose* Key Understandings

- *Summarize the main idea of the story.*
  - Duck and Goose make a false hypothesis that what they've found is an egg. They get into multiple arguments and even question their friendship, only to find out the "egg" is a ball.
- *Does this book show scientific thinking? Explain.*
  - No, Duck and Goose create a hypothesis, but don't conduct a controlled experiment to determine if their hypothesis is correct. They only assume their idea is correct.
- *What observations do Duck and Goose make to determine the ball was an "egg"?*
  - The item is round and rolls.
- *How can linear thinking lead us astray?*
  - If we draw a conclusion without going through the steps of an experiment, our conclusion may be wrong.

### Skill Development Activity

- Have students take out their Scientific Method Flip Book. Remind students that the scientific method provides a framework to conduct experiments.
- Explain that after conducting an experiment, scientists must share their results.
- Tell students they will be writing up the results of their experiment. Guide the students through summarizing their results. If students require scaffolding, use this cloze writing activity. See Box 5.4 for sample solutions.

## Box 5.4: Share Your Results

- According to my experiment, the apple is best preserved (dependent variable) using the *lemon juice* (independent variable). The apple slices were observed at the *5-minute, 10-minute, and 30-minute marks*. My hypothesis was that if the apple was put in *milk, then it would preserve the apple because milk has vitamins and minerals*. My results *do not support* my hypothesis. I think

# ANALYTICAL THINKING for Advanced Learners, Grades 3–5

> that my test *did go smoothly* because *I was careful to watch the time and wrote good observation notes*. Something I wonder now is *would all citrus juices work to preserve the apple's coloring?* An interesting future study might involve *trying grapefruit juice and lime juice instead of lemon.*

## Investigate and Reflect Authentic Application Activity: Analytical Thinking Code Breaker

**Objective:** Apply all the analytical thinking skills to break the code.

### Materials

- Handout 5.6: Analytical Thinker: Code Breaker

Prepare the Analytical Thinker: Code Breaker booklet (Handout 5.6) for each student.

- Copy each page single sided or print from www.routledge.com/97810 32199269.
- Fold the front/back cover in half. The crease should be on the left side of the front cover.
- Fold each of the inner pages in half with the text facing outward. The crease should be on the right side of the even-numbered pages.
- Stack folded book pages so that even page numbers are stacked sequentially facing the top, starting with page 2.
- Place the stack of folded interior pages inside of the folded cover page. Loose edges should be against the cover's fold, with the creased edge of the internal pages facing outward.
- Staple along the left-hand side, using the provided staple lines as a guide.
- If desired, place a strip of tape along the left-hand side to cover the staples, trimming any excess.

### Whole Group Introduction

- Ask students: What does it mean to be an analytical thinker? Students should be able to state the five sub-skills of analytical thinking. Prompt students to explain what each sub-skill means.
- Ask students: Can you take this information to the next level and apply the knowledge to solve the following puzzles and discover the codes?

# I DID IT!

Record the **FINAL CODES** for each section below.

| Noticing Details | |
| --- | --- |
| Ask Questions | |
| Classify & Organize | |
| Make a Hypothesis | |
| Investigate & Reflect | |

Handout 5.6 Analytical Thinker Code Breaker

# ANALYTICAL THINKING
## CODE BREAKER

*Think like a RESEARCHER to break the CODE*

Researcher's Name:

# THINK LIKE A RESEARCHER...

It's time to put your **Analytical Thinking Skills** to use. You have learned to apply logical thinking to break down complex ideas into smaller parts in order to solve a problem. Can you take this knowledge to the next level and apply these skills to solve these challenge puzzles?

Get ready to:
1. Notice Details
2. Ask Questions
3. Classify and Organize
4. Make a Hypothesis
5. Think and Think Again

Be sure to record all the **FINAL CODES** on the last page.

---

# NOTICING DETAILS
### LOOKING FOR ATTRIBUTES AND IMPORTANT TRAITS

**Shape and Number Sudoku 1**

Look at the logic puzzles below. The puzzle is completed, each column and row has exactly one of each shape and one of each number.

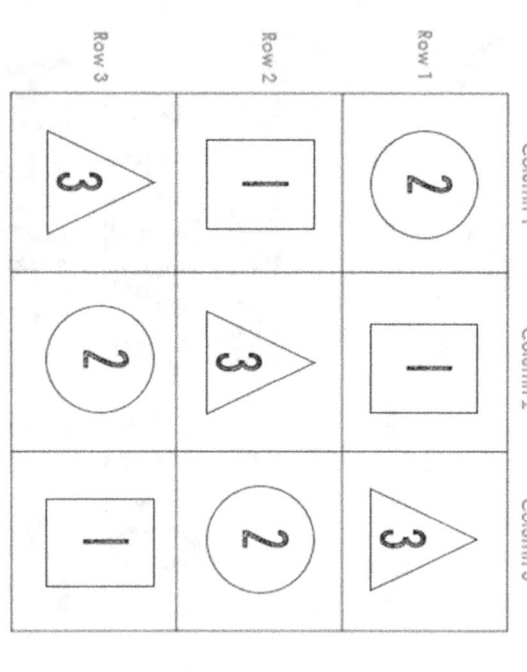

|  | Column 1 | Column 2 | Column 3 |
|---|---|---|---|
| Row 1 | 2 (circle) | 1 (square) | 3 (triangle) |
| Row 2 | 1 (square) | 3 (triangle) | 2 (circle) |
| Row 3 | 3 (triangle) | 2 (circle) | 1 (square) |

# NOTICING DETAILS
## LOOKING FOR ATTRIBUTES AND IMPORTANT TRAITS

### Shape and Number Sudoku 2

Complete the logic puzzle by drawing the shapes and recording the correct numbers. Remember each column and row must have exactly one of each shape and one of each number.

|  | Column 1 | Column 2 | Column 3 | Column 4 |
|---|---|---|---|---|
| Row 1 | ☐ 2 |  | △ 3 | ⬔ 4 |
| Row 2 |  |  | ○ 1 |  |
| Row 3 | ○ 1 | ☐ 2 |  |  |
| Row 4 |  |  |  | ☐ 2 |

# FIGURE OUT THE CODE
## NOTICING DETAILS FINAL CODE

Record the numbers from left to right from the 1st row and 3rd row. Then add them together to get the FINAL CODE.

Sudoku Row 1: _ _ _ _

➕

Sudoku Row 3: _ _ _ _

═

**FINAL CODE :** _ _ _ _

# ASKING QUESTIONS
## WONDERING ABOUT OUR WORLD

### What's my RULE 1?
Look at the groups of words below, what is the rule to fit in the group?

| In the word club | NOT in the word club |
|---|---|
| radar   civic   kayak | sports   roast   sports |
| level   racecar   mom | boat   look   ruler |

Circle the words in the word club.

| 1. card | 2. child | 3. dad | 4. Anna | 5. frog |
|---|---|---|---|---|
| 6. wow | 7. student | 8. solos | 9. star | 10. world |

What is my RULE 1?

**CODE 1:** Write the numbers of the words that fit the RULE in numerical order: ___ , ___ , ___ , ___ , ___

Handout 5.6 Analytical Thinker Code Breaker

5

---

# ASKING QUESTIONS
## WONDERING ABOUT OUR WORLD

### What's my RULE 2?
Look at the groups of words below, what is the rule to fit in the group?

| In the word club | NOT in the word club |
|---|---|
| act   heart   part | chain   look   rule |
| tea   ape   listen | many   boat   frog |

Circle the words in the word club.

| 1. aide | 2. many | 3. card | 4. tar | 5. flow |
|---|---|---|---|---|
| 6. child | 7. stop | 8. sing | 9. egg | 10. world |

What is my RULE 2?

**CODE 2:** Write the numbers of the words that fit the RULE in numerical order: ___ , ___ , ___ , ___ , ___

Handout 5.6 Analytical Thinker Code Breaker

# FIGURE OUT THE CODE

## ASKING QUESTIONS FINAL CODE

Record the numbers from left to right from the 1st row and 3rd row.
Then add them together to get the FINAL CODE.

Rule 1 Code: ____

Rule 2 Code: ____

FINAL CODE: ___ ___ ___ ___

---

# CLASSIFY & ORGANIZE
## GROUPING INFORMATION IN A MEANIGFUL WAY

### Divisible Sets 1

Look at the numbers in the box below. They can all be evenly divided by 2 or by 3. Some can be evenly divided by both 2 and 3. Write the numbers in the correct spot on the Venn diagram.

| 58 | 16 | 42 | 9  | 21 |
|----|----|----|----|----|
| 36 | 27 | 18 | 48 | 44 |
| 45 | 60 | 39 | 62 | 34 |

Divisible by 2 — Divisible by 2 & 3 — Divisible by 3

# CLASSIFY & ORGANIZE
## GROUPING INFORMATION IN A MEANINGFUL WAY

### Divisible Sets 2

Look at the numbers in the box below. They can all be evenly divided by 2 or by 5. Some can be evenly divided by both 2 and 5. Write the numbers in the correct spot on the Venn diagram.

| 12 | 15 | 10 | 40 | 22 |
|----|----|----|----|----|
| 35 | 75 | 50 | 36 | 42 |
| 60 | 55 | 25 | 80 | 38 |

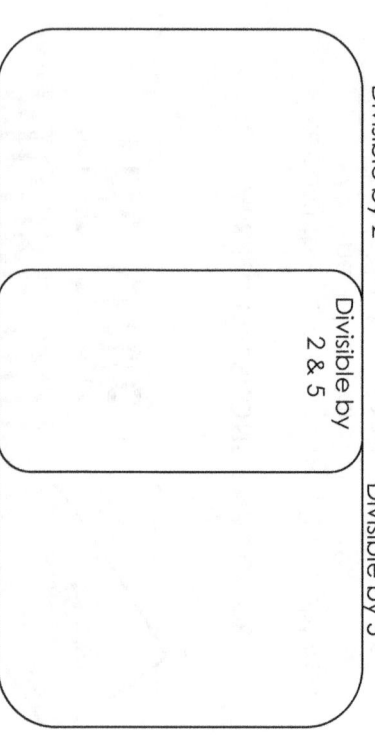

Divisible by 2     Divisible by 2 & 5     Divisible by 5

Handout 5.6 Analytical Thinker Code Breaker    9

---

# FIGURE OUT THE CODE

## CLASSIFY & ORGANIZE FINAL CODE

Look at the numbers in the box below. They can all be evenly divided by 2, 3 or by 5. Some can be evenly divided by 2, 3, and/or 5. Write the numbers in the correct spot on the Venn diagram.

| 12 | 15 | 10 | 40 | 22 |
|----|----|----|----|----|
| 35 | 75 | 50 | 36 | 42 |
| 60 | 55 | 25 | 80 | 38 |

**EVENLY DIVISIBLE BY:**

2    2 & 5    2 & 3    2, 3, & 5    3    3 & 5    5

**FINAL CODE:** Record the numbers in the divisible by all section in reverse numerical order.

_____  _____  _____

Handout 5.6 Analytical Thinker Code Breaker    10

# MAKE A HYPOTHESIS
## PREDICTING BASED ON WHAT WE KNOW

### Number Patterns 1

A **magic square** is made up of numbers arranged so that all the numbers in each row, column, and diagonal add up to the same sum. This sum is called the magic number. Solve the magic square below.

**MAGIC NUMBER: 34**

| 13 |    |    | 1  |
|----|----|----|----|
| 3  |    |    | 15 |
|    |    | 7  |    |
| 16 | 5  |    | 4  |

---

# MAKE A HYPOTHESIS
## PREDICTING BASED ON WHAT WE KNOW

### Number Patterns 2

Each shape in the grid has a value between 1 and 9, the total of each horizontal row is shown.

**How much is each shape worth?**

|   |   |   |   |     |
|---|---|---|---|-----|
| ☺ | ♥ | ♥ | ⚡ | = 24 |
| ☺ | ⚡ | ♥ | ★ | = 23 |
| ★ | ⚡ | ♥ | ♥ | = 20 |
| ★ | ⚡ | ♥ | ★ | = 19 |

 = 

 = 

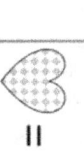 = 

 =

# FIGURE OUT THE CODE

Use the numbers from the Number Pattern 2 to complete the math equations below. The answers will be your CODE.

1st number: ⭐ x 2 =

2nd number: 12 − 😊 =

3rd number: ❤️ + 😊 − ⚡ =

4th number: ⚡ + ❤️ − 😊 =

**FINAL CODE**
Record the numbers in order:
___ ___ ___ ___

---

# INVESTIGATE & REFLECT
## EXAMINING DATA TO DRAW CONCLUSIONS

On Oak Street there are four houses. Follow the clues to figure out who & what lives in each house.

**House Colors:** red, green, blue, yellow, green
**Nationalities:** American, Brazilian, Canadian, Australian
**Pets:** dog, cat, fish, bird
**Jobs:** doctor, teacher, lawyer, architect

| House # | 1 | 2 | 3 | 4 |
|---|---|---|---|---|
| Color | | | | |
| Nationality | | | | |
| Pet | | | | |
| Job | | | | |

# INVESTIGATE & REFLECT
## EXAMINING DATA TO DRAW CONCLUSIONS

1. The Canadian lives in the second house.
2. The green house is next door to the red house.
3. The teacher lives between the lawyer and the architect in that order.
4. The owner of the green house is a doctor.
5. The Australian is a doctor.
6. The teacher lives exactly to the left of the red house.
7. The American lives exactly to the left of the man who has fish.
8. The dog owner lives in the 2nd house.
9. The American lives in the red house.
10. The person living in the third house loves birds.
11. The doctor lives to the right of the person with birds.
12. The person who lives in the blue house live next door to the lawyer.

# FIGURE OUT THE CODE

Record the house numbers below.

The red house is number: _____

The fish lives in house number: _____

The Canadian lives in house number: _____

The lawyer lives in house number: _____

**FINAL CODE:** _____

❏ Distribute the student Analytical Thinking: Code Breaker booklet (Handout 5.6). Depending upon your student population, this may be done independently, in partners, or as a whole group. The following directions have the teacher explaining the skill and then allowing students time to complete each section before moving on to the next puzzle. This can be broken up into multiple sessions depending upon your student population.

❏ Make sure students complete each puzzle and show you their responses before moving on to the next. Continue until all puzzles have been solved.

❏ **Noticing Details:** Review the Noticing Details Anchor Chart. Explain that in this section, students will be looking for important attributes to complete the Shape and Number Sudoku puzzles.
   1. Students should study the Shape and Number Sudoku puzzle 1 (booklet page 2), while teacher explains, "The logic puzzles below are completed when each column and row has exactly one of each shape and one of each number." Show the students how the shape and number remain together in the matrix grid.
   2. Next, students will complete the Shape and Number Sudoku 2 (booklet page 3). Students will draw the correct shape in the matrix grid and label the shape with the correct number (see Figure 5.1).
   3. To complete the Noticing Details code (booklet page 4), students must record the four numbers from left to right from the first and third row of the booklet page, and then add them together to get the Noticing Details Final Code (see Figure 5.2).
   4. Students should record the final code on the back of the book.

❏ **Asking Questions:** Review the Asking Questions Anchor Chart. Explain that in this section, students will be wondering about the world of words. Students will need to observe the groups of words in the word club and the group of words *not* in the word club.
   1. Introduce What's my Rule 1? on booklet page 5. Ask students what they notice about the words in the word club. Ask students what they notice about words *not* in the word club.
   2. Students should notice that the words in the word club can be read forward and backward. Introduce the term *palindrome*, which is a word spelled the same forward and backward. Tell students to circle the palindromes from the chart. Next, students will write the numbers of the words that fit Rule 1 in numerical order on the bottom of the page (see Figure 5.3).
   3. Tell students to look at What's my Rule 2? on booklet page 6. Ask students to look carefully at the words in the word club and those *not* in the word club. Allow students time to grapple with how the words are alike. If they can't come up with the right answer, give

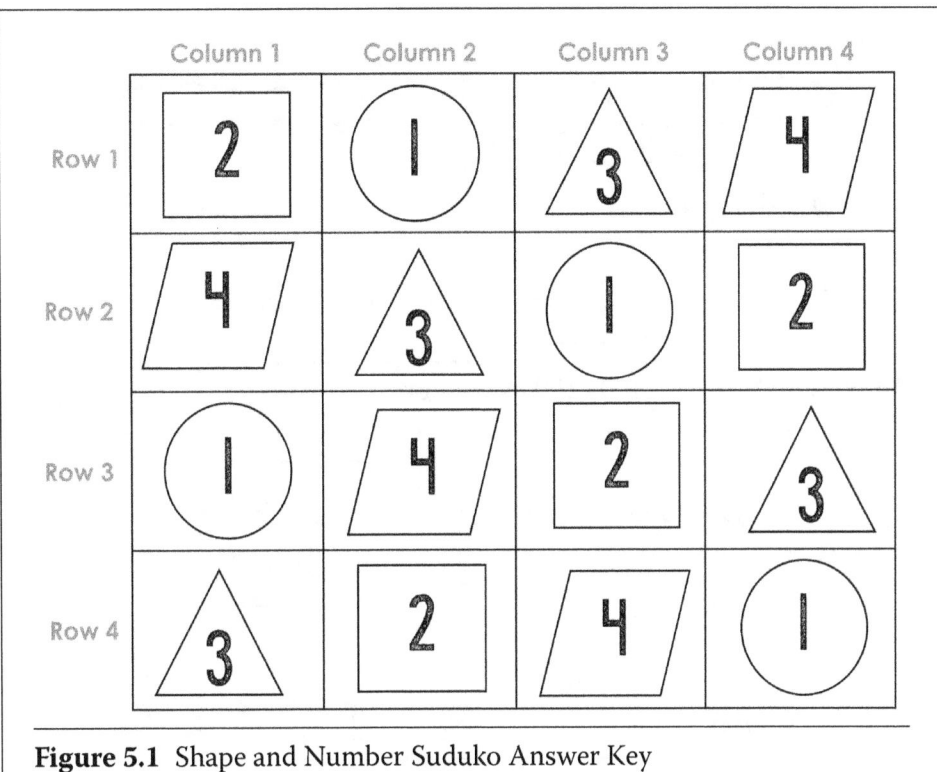

**Figure 5.1** Shape and Number Suduko Answer Key

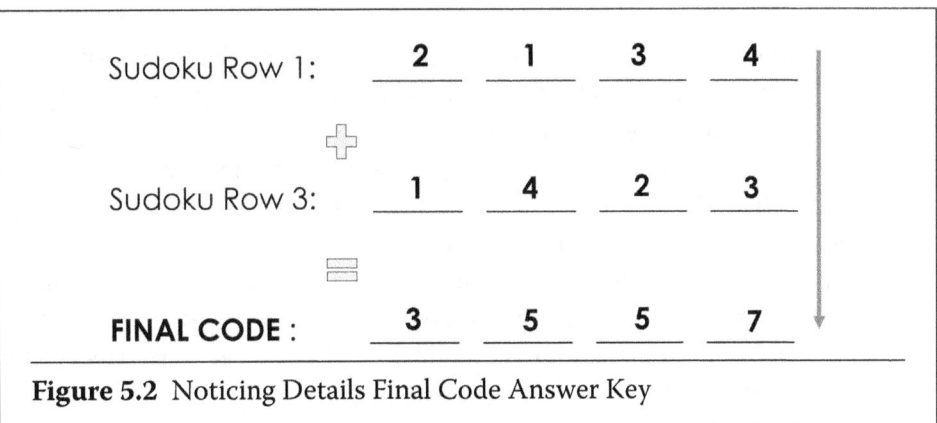

**Figure 5.2** Noticing Details Final Code Answer Key

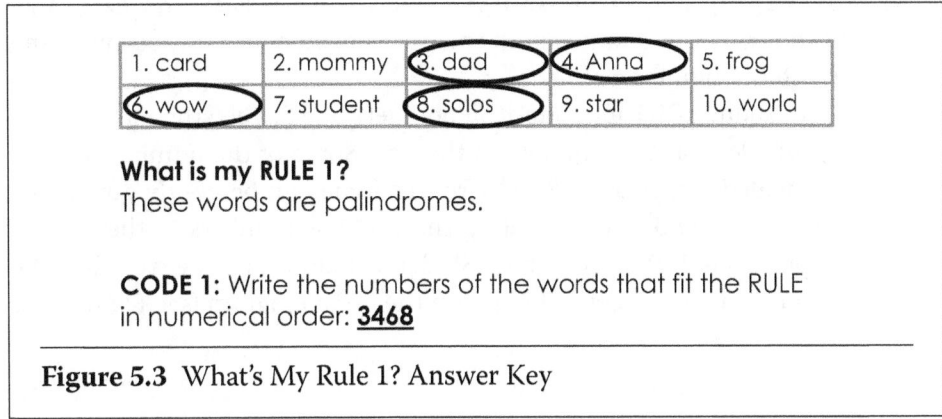

**Figure 5.3** What's My Rule 1? Answer Key

# ANALYTICAL THINKING for Advanced Learners, Grades 3–5

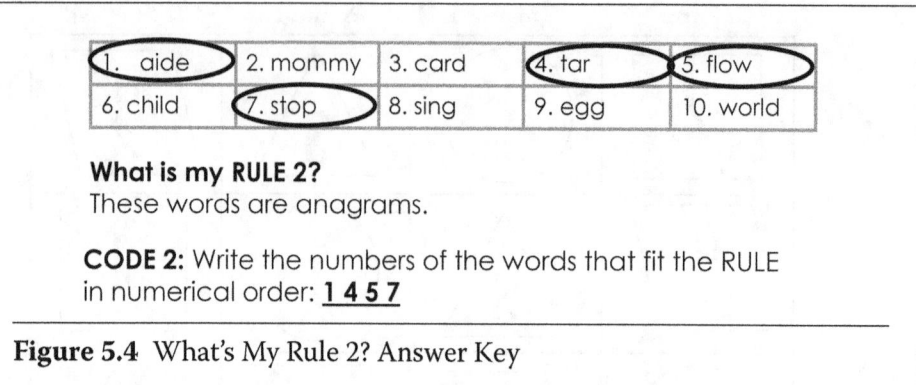

Figure 5.4  What's My Rule 2? Answer Key

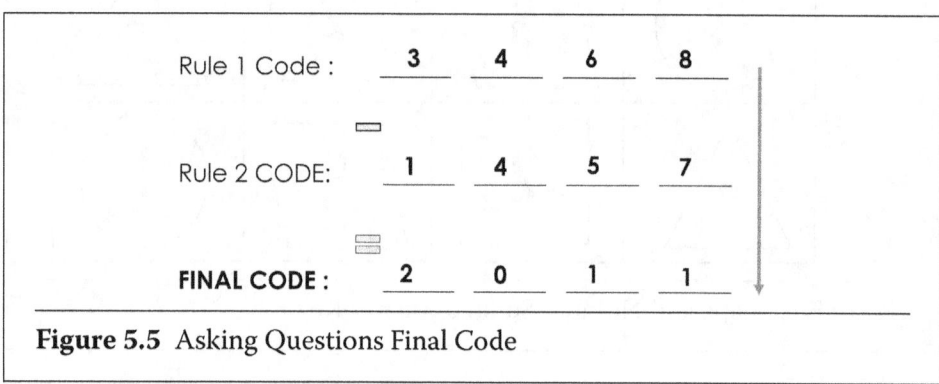

Figure 5.5  Asking Questions Final Code

students a hint by showing how to rearrange the letters of *act* to form *cat*. Explain that the words you can make by rearranging the letters are called anagrams.

4. Tell students to circle the anagrams from the chart. Next, students will write the numbers of the words that fit Rule 2 in numerical order on the bottom of the page (see Figure 5.4).
5. To complete the Asking Questions code (page 7), students must record the four numbers from left to right from the first Rule and second Rule, and then subtract them to get the Answering Questions Final Code (see Figure 5.5).
6. Students should record the final code on the back of the book.

❑ **Classifying and Organizing:** Review the Classify and Organize Anchor Chart. Explain that in this section, students will be analyzing divisibility number patterns.

1. Introduce Divisible Sets 1 on booklet page 8. Tell students to carefully look at the numbers in the box. Some of the numbers can be divided *evenly* by two *or* by three. Some can be *evenly* divided by both 2 *and* 3. Model writing the first few numbers in the correct places on the Venn diagram. Students should continue recording the numbers in the correct place on the Venn diagram (see Figure 5.6).

# Sub-Skill 5

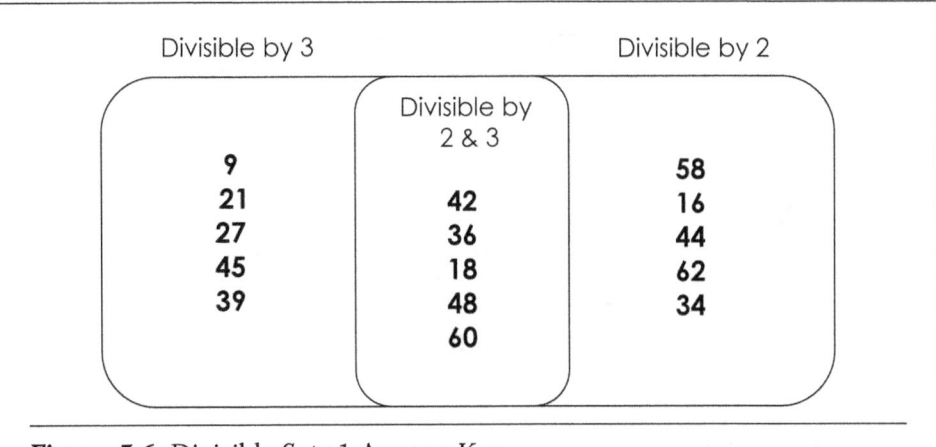

**Figure 5.6** Divisible Sets 1 Answer Key

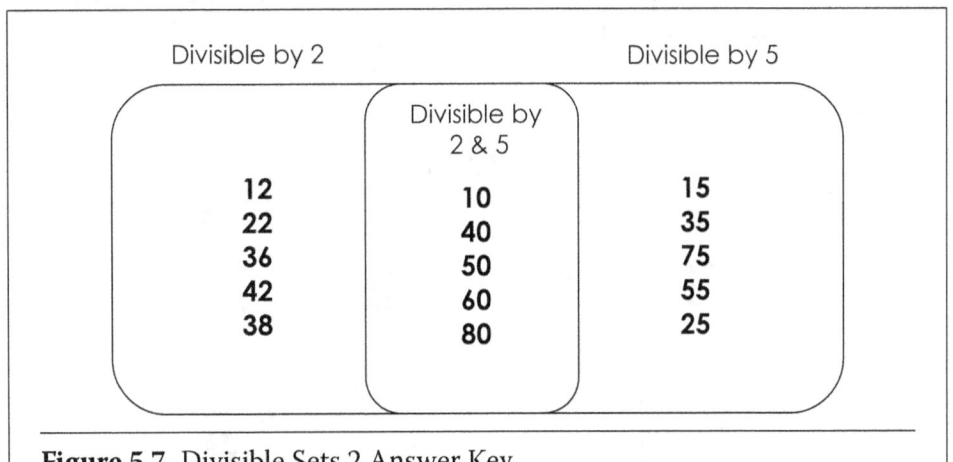

**Figure 5.7** Divisible Sets 2 Answer Key

2. Tell students to follow the same procedure with Divisible Sets 2 (page 9).
3. To complete the Classify and Organize final code, students must complete a three-way Venn diagram. The numbers in the middle of the Venn diagram should be recorded as the code in reverse numerical order (see Figure 5.7).
   - Modify this as you see fit for your student population. Some students may understand the concept, and others may need heavy modeling to complete.
4. Students should record the final code on the back of the book (see Figure 5.8).

❑ **Make a Hypothesis:** Review the Make a Hypothesis Anchor Chart. Explain that in this section, students will be making educated guesses based on the information known.
   1. Introduce Number Patterns 1 (page 11). Explain that a magic square is made up of numbers arranged so that all the numbers in each

# ANALYTICAL THINKING for Advanced Learners, Grades 3–5

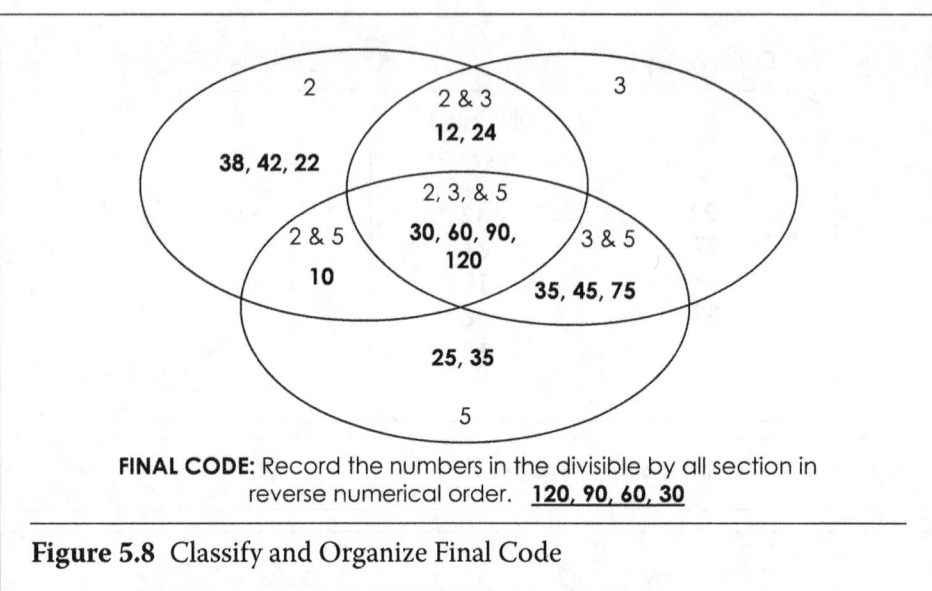

**FINAL CODE:** Record the numbers in the divisible by all section in reverse numerical order.  **120, 90, 60, 30**

**Figure 5.8** Classify and Organize Final Code

**MAGIC NUMBER: 34**

| 13 | 8  | 12 | 1  |
|----|----|----|----|
| 3  | 10 | 6  | 15 |
| 2  | 11 | 7  | 14 |
| 16 | 5  | 9  | 4  |

**Figure 5.9** Magic Square Answer Key

row, column, and diagonal add up to the same sum. This sum is called the magic number. See Figure 5.9.

2. Show students how to use the information given to make hypotheses to complete the magic square. Remind students to start with the row or column with the most information.

Sub-Skill 5

☺ = 8    ★ = 4    ♥ = 5    ⚡ = 6

**Figure 5.10** Number Pattern 2 Answer Key

1st number: ★ x 2 = **8**

2nd number: 12 - ☺ = **4**

3rd number: ♥ + ☺ - ⚡ = **7**

4th number: ⚡ + ♥ - ☺ = **3**

**FINAL CODE**
Record the numbers in order: **8, 4, 7, 3**

**Figure 5.11** Make a Hypothesis Final Code

3. Introduce Number Patterns 2 (page 12). Explain that in this type of grid, each shape has a value between 1 and 9. The total of each horizontal check strategy to determine the values of each shape (see Figure 5.10).
4. To complete the Make a Hypothesis Final Code, students must use the corresponding shape values to complete each math equation. The answers in order will be the final code (see Figure 5.11).
5. Students should record the final code on the back of the book.

❏ **Investigate and Reflect:** Review the Investigate and Reflect Anchor Chart. Explain that in this section, students will be completing a modified puzzle created by Albert Einstein (see Figure 5.12 for the final solution to this puzzle).

1. Show the students the matrix and explain how to record the answers. Tell students they will need to read through the clues multiple times. Read through the clues together (page 15). Ask students what answers they know *for sure* based on the clues. Model completing the corresponding squares (see Table 5.2).
   - *The Canadian lives in house two.*
   - *The Brazilian lives in house one.*
   - *The second house is blue.*
   - *The fourth house is green.*
   - *The dog lives in the blue house.*
2. Next, tell students to re-read the clues to see if they can determine other answers based on what they have filled in. Make sure they use a pencil, as they may need to change their answers (see Table 5.3).

# ANALYTICAL THINKING for Advanced Learners, Grades 3–5

**Investigate and Reflect Riddle**

| House # | 1 | 2 | 3 | 4 |
|---|---|---|---|---|
| Color | yellow | blue | red | green |
| Nationality | Brazilian | Canadian | American | Australian |
| Pet | cat | dog | bird | fish |
| Job | lawyer | teacher | architect | doctor |

The red house is number: **3**
The fish lives in house number: **4**
The Canadian lives in house number: **2**
The lawyer lives in house number: **1**

**Investigate and Reflect FINAL CODE: 3421**

**Figure 5.12** Investigate and Reflect Riddle

## TABLE 5.2
Think and Think Again Initial Clues

| House # | 1 | 2 | 3 | 4 |
|---|---|---|---|---|
| color | | blue | | green |
| nationality | Brazilian | Canadian | | |
| pet | | dog | | |
| job | | | | |

## TABLE 5.3
Think and Think Again Secondary Clues

| House # | 1 | 2 | 3 | 4 |
|---|---|---|---|---|
| color | yellow | blue | red | green |
| nationality | Brazilian | Canadian | American | |
| pet | cat | dog | | |
| job | lawyer | | architect | |

- *The first house is not red.* If we know the first house isn't red, it must be yellow.
- *The architect lives directly next to the green house.* Since we know the fourth house is green, the architect must live in the third house.
- *The dog owner lives to the right of the cat owner.* Since the dog lives in house two, then the cat must live in house one.
- *The dog owner lives to the right of the lawyer.* The lawyer must be in house one for the dog owner to live on the right side of him.
- *The Canadian lives directly next to the American.* Therefore, the American lives in house three.
- *The Australian is a doctor.* This leaves the fourth house to the Australian doctor.
- *The Brazilian lives directly next to the teacher.* So, the teacher is the Canadian in house two.
- *The bird owner lives directly next to the teacher.* Therefore, the bird lives in the third house and the fish must live in the fourth.

Record the **FINAL CODES** for each section below.

| Noticing Details | 3557 |
|---|---|
| Ask Questions | 2011 |
| Classify and Organize | 120,906,030 |
| Make a Hypothesis | 8473 |
| Investigate & Reflect | 3421 |

**Figure 5.13** I Did It! Code Breaker

## Investigate and Reflect Concluding Activities

- ❏ Distribute the Investigate and Reflect Exit Ticket (Appendix A). Ask students to reflect on their learning about the skill of examining data to draw conclusions. Allow time for students to complete the exit ticket. Use this as a formative assessment to gain a better understanding of your students' readiness to effectively practice the skill.
- ❏ If desired, complete the Group Investigate and Reflect Rubric (Appendix A) to track students' progress with the skill.
- ❏ If desired, use the Analytical Thinking Student Observation Rubric (Appendix A) to assess and quantify individual students' mastery.
- ❏ Ask students to retrieve their Analytical Thinking Avatar (Handout I.4). In the "Investigate and Reflect" box, they should either write the main ideas of this section or illustrate their avatar using the skills of investigating and reflecting.

## Bibliography

Hills, T. (2006). *Duck & goose.* New York: Schwartz & Wade, A Random House Company.

Offill, J. (2011). *11 Experiments that failed.* New York: Schwartz & Wade, A Penguin Random House Company.

# Appendix A

## *Assessments*

Several assessment options are provided in this unit. It is not necessary to use all the options provided; rather, you should choose the options that work best for your own classroom needs.

One aspect to pay close attention to is the indicators associated with each thinking skill. These indicators provide an outline of expected behavioral outcomes for students. As you work through the lessons, keep an eye out for students who are able to achieve the indicators efficiently and effectively, as well as those who may need more support. The intent of this unit is to foster a mastery mindset; make note of student growth and skill development as you progress, rather than focusing on summative outcomes against specific benchmarks.

1. **Exit Tickets:** Exit tickets are provided to correspond with each sub-skill. These are intended to be formative, giving you a sense of students' mastery and self-efficacy with each skill. These tickets will also give you great insight into areas where a re-visit is warranted. If a student would benefit from additional instruction in a sub-skill area, consider using one or more of the extension options listed in Appendix B.
2. **Individual Student Observations:** This form is intended for use for each student individually. All five thinking skills are outlined on the page, and you can track individual student progress toward indicator goals easily. Use this form to gather data, report data to stakeholders, or simply help students see their own progress.

# ANALYTICAL THINKING for Advanced Learners, Grades 3–5

3. **Analytical Thinking Sub-Skill Group Observation Checklists:** This checklist is provided for each thinking skill. This is a great running measure of students' mastery of the indicators associated with each thinking skill. Each skill has three indicators for mastery, and you can track student progress toward these goals as a group using this form.

## Handout A.1: Noticing Details Exit Ticket

Name: _____
Date: _____

Noticing Details is…

The easiest part about noticing details is…

The trickiest part about noticing details is…

How confident I feel about my ability to notice details:

Your opinion (feelings, questions, ideas, favorite parts) of this unit:

# Handout A.2: Asking Questions Exit Ticket

Name: _____

Date: _____

What does it mean to ask good questions?

The easiest part about asking questions is…

The trickiest part about asking questions is…

How confident I feel about my ability to ask questions.

Your opinion (feelings, questions, ideas, favorite parts) of this unit:

## Handout A.3: Classify & Organize Exit Ticket

Name: _____
Date: _____

What does it mean to classify and organize?

The easiest part about classifying and organizing is…

The trickiest part about classifying and organizing is…

How confident I feel about my ability to classify and organize is…

Your opinion (feelings, questions, ideas, favorite parts) of this unit:

**Handout A.4:** Make a Hypothesis Exit Ticket

Name: _____
Date: _____

What does it mean to make a hypothesis?

The easiest part about making a hypothesis is…

The trickiest part about making a hypothesis is…

How confident I feel about my ability to make a hypothesis.

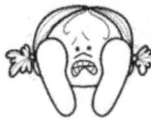   

Your opinion (feelings, questions, ideas, favorite parts) of this unit:

# Handout A.5: Investigate & Reflect Exit Ticket

Name: _____
Date: _____

What does it mean to investigate and reflect?

The easiest part about investigating and reflecting is…

The trickiest part about investigating and reflecting is…

How confident I feel about my ability to investigate.

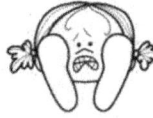   

Your opinion (feelings, questions, ideas, favorite parts) of this unit:

# Handout A.6: Individual Student Observation Rubric

| Masterful | Exceeds expectations |
|---|---|
| Proficient | Independent mastery |
| Developing | Success with scaffolding |
| Beginning | Not yet achieved |

Student name:

| | MASTERFUL (4) | PROFICIENT (3) | DEVELOPING (2) | BEGINNING (1) |
|---|---|---|---|---|
| **NOTICING DETAILS**<br>• Note and fully describe both large and small details<br>• Differentiate between essential and nonessential details<br>• Attend to differences in characteristics | | | | |
| Notes: | | | | |
| **ASKING QUESTIONS**<br>• Compare and contrast ideas/topics<br>• Generates questions based on observations<br>• Identifies knowns vs. unknowns | | | | |
| Notes: | | | | |
| **CLASSIFY & ORGANIZE**<br>• Group information based on criteria given<br>• Develop criteria for organization<br>• Analyze areas of overlap in classification | | | | |
| Notes: | | | | |
| **MAKE A HYPOTHESIS**<br>• Make predictions about outcomes<br>• Uses prior knowledge to make educated guesses<br>• Generate testable inquiry statements | | | | |
| Notes: | | | | |
| **INVESTIGATE & REFLECT**<br>• Revisit problems to revise solution paths<br>• Generalize thinking to develop rules<br>• Verify results through multiple testing opportunities | | | | |
| Notes: | | | | |

# Handout A.7: Noticing Details Group Checklist

| * | Exceeds expectations |
|---|---|
| + | Independent mastery |
| ✓ | Success with scaffolding |
| o | Not yet achieved |

| Students | Indicators | | |
|---|---|---|---|
| | Note and fully describe large and small details | Differentiate between essential and nonessential details | Attend to differences in characteristics |
| | | | |
| | | | |
| | | | |
| | | | |
| | | | |
| | | | |
| | | | |
| | | | |
| | | | |
| | | | |
| | | | |
| | | | |
| | | | |
| | | | |
| | | | |
| | | | |

# Handout A.8: Asking Questions Group Checklist

| | |
|---|---|
| * | Exceeds expectations |
| + | Independent mastery |
| ✓ | Success with scaffolding |
| o | Not yet achieved |

| Students | Indicators | | |
|---|---|---|---|
| | Compare and contrast ideas/topics | Generates questions based on observations | Identifies knowns versus unknowns |
| | | | |
| | | | |
| | | | |
| | | | |
| | | | |
| | | | |
| | | | |
| | | | |
| | | | |
| | | | |
| | | | |
| | | | |
| | | | |
| | | | |
| | | | |
| | | | |
| | | | |

# Handout A.9: Classify & Organize Group Checklist

| * | Exceeds expectations |
|---|---|
| + | Independent mastery |
| ✓ | Success with scaffolding |
| o | Not yet achieved |

| Students | Indicators | | |
|---|---|---|---|
| | Group information based on criteria given | Develops own criteria for organization | Analyze areas of overlap in classification |
| | | | |
| | | | |
| | | | |
| | | | |
| | | | |
| | | | |
| | | | |
| | | | |
| | | | |
| | | | |
| | | | |
| | | | |
| | | | |
| | | | |
| | | | |
| | | | |

# Handout A.10: Make a Hypothesis Group Checklist

| * | Exceeds expectations |
|---|---|
| + | Independent mastery |
| ✓ | Success with scaffolding |
| o | Not yet achieved |

| Students | Indicators | | |
|---|---|---|---|
| | Make predictions about outcomes | Uses prior knowledge to make educated guesses | Generates testable inquiry statement |
| | | | |
| | | | |
| | | | |
| | | | |
| | | | |
| | | | |
| | | | |
| | | | |
| | | | |
| | | | |
| | | | |
| | | | |
| | | | |
| | | | |
| | | | |
| | | | |
| | | | |

# Handout A.11: Investigate and Reflect Group Checklist

| * | Exceeds expectations |
|---|---|
| + | Independent mastery |
| ✓ | Success with scaffolding |
| o | Not yet achieved |

| Students | Indicators | | |
|---|---|---|---|
| | Revisit problems to revise solution paths | Generalize thinking to develop rules | Verify results through multiple testing opportunities |
| | | | |
| | | | |
| | | | |
| | | | |
| | | | |
| | | | |
| | | | |
| | | | |
| | | | |
| | | | |
| | | | |
| | | | |
| | | | |
| | | | |
| | | | |
| | | | |
| | | | |

# Appendix B

## *Extensions*

### Alternate Trade Books

In some cases, not all the trade books referenced within this unit may be readily available, or they may not be suited for your classroom environment, preferences, or audience. In other cases, you may choose to expand or deepen student understanding through an additional example rooted in rich text. Books listed in Table B.1 are suggestions for further study or to take the place of any of the read-aloud trade books suggested throughout the unit. Also included is a blackline master Read Aloud Reflection (Handout B.1), which can be used with any book of your choice to target the specified thinking skill.

**TABLE B.1**
Suggested Alternate Trade Books

| Analytical Thinking Sub-Skill | Suggested Alternate Trade Books/Guiding Questions |
|---|---|
| Noticing Details | ❏ *Enigma* by Graeme Base (Can you find all the lost objects and observe the secret code?)<br>❏ *The Lost House* by B. B. Cronin (How does color affect our ability to easily observe?)<br>❏ *Nothing Ever Happens on 90th Street* by Roni Schotter (What events do we fail to notice if we aren't looking for them?) |
| Asking Questions | ❏ *Animalogies* by Scholastic (How do the students make connections by asking questions?)<br>❏ *Beach Is to Fun: A Book of Relationships* by Pat Brisson (How are ___ and ___ alike? How are they different?)<br>❏ *Duck Rabbit* by Amy Rosenthal and Tom Lichtenheld (This optical illusion book requires students to change their perspective to determine if the image is a duck or a rabbit.)<br>❏ *Cece Loves Science* by Kimberly Derting and Shelli R. Johannes (Cece loves to ask questions, and through encouragement from her teacher, learns that "Science isn't just about asking questions…real scientists have fun finding answers too.") |
| Classifying and Organizing | ❏ *A Little Bit of Oomph!* by Barnie Saltzberg (Adding a little oomph turns the ordinary, extraordinary.)<br>❏ *Bad Day At Riverbend* by Chris Van Allsburg (This adventure begins as a black and white story but then the crayons attack and elaborate the story with color.)<br>❏ *Big Frog Can't Fit In* by Mo Willems (In this "pop-out" book, a poor Big Frog just can't fit into the book.)<br>❏ *Sector 7* by David Wiesner (A boy discovers a gateway into the cloud factory in the sky.) |
| Make a Hypothesis | ❏ *Who Done It?* by Olivier Tallec (Students will use context clues to make a hypothesis.)<br>❏ *I Want My Hat Back* and/or *We Found a Hat* by Jon Klassen (Very similar in style to *This is Not My Hat*, but with an added need to observe each illustration closely.)<br>❏ *A Hungry Lion, or a Dwindling Assortment of Animals* by Lucy Ruth Cummins (Where do all of Lion's friends keep disappearing to?)<br>❏ *Ring! Yo?* by Chris Raschka (Can you infer what is happening on the other side of the phone call?)<br>❏ *Scampers Thinks Like a Scientist* by Mike Allegra (Scampers the mouse goes through a series of hypotheses to make a deduction and shares her conclusion with her friends.) |
| Investigate and Reflect | ❏ *Guess Again* by Mac Barnett (How can we use clues to make a hypothesis? How can linear thinking lead us astray?)<br>❏ *The Princess and the Petri Dish* by Sue Fliess (Pippa the princess uses the scientific method to improve the taste of peas.) |

# Handout B.1: Universal Read Aloud Reflection
*Book Title:*

Name: _____

| Summarize the main idea of the story. | How did the book connect to the focus skill? |
|---|---|
| | |

What details from the text showcase the focus skill?

What patterns do you notice in your list from the question above?

What generalization (big idea) can you make about the focus skill based on this book?

## Novel Study Extensions

Novels are a great way to extend learning about thinking skills, applying analytical thinking in a broader context. The novels listed below support the thinking skills of this unit. The novel study units will allow the students to apply the thinking skills while reading excellent literature.

*Mrs. Frisby and the Rats of NIMH* by Robert C. O'Brien

Mrs. Frisby is a widowed mouse with four small children. Each summer they must move out of the field or face almost certain death. Her youngest child, Timothy, is ill with pneumonia and cannot be moved until he is healthy. Fortunately, the rats of NIMH, a group of extremely intelligent rats, agree to help her and come up with a brilliant solution to her dilemma.

- ❏ This novel study encourages readers to analyze text on a deeper level, develop their critical thinking skills, and gain an understanding of theme and descriptive language.

*Fantastic Mr. Fox* by Roald Dahl

A thief has been stealing from the farmers and they know who the culprit is … Fantastic Mr. Fox. The farmers join forces to outwit Mr. Fox, and they have his family surrounded. Fortunately, this is not just any fox…this is Fantastic Mr. Fox. Can he create a plan fantastic enough to save his family?

- ❏ This novel study encourages readers to analyze text on a deeper level, develop their critical thinking skills, and think, infer, and cite text evidence to support their answers. They will also need to be organized in their reading approach.

*The One and Only Ivan* By Katherine Applegate

The One and Only Ivan is a fiction novel about a gorilla named Ivan who tries to piece together his past with the help of an elephant named Stella, as they hatch a plan to escape from captivity.

- ❏ The focus of this unit is to guide students to analyze text on a deeper level, gaining rich understandings of theme and descriptive language. Students will need to think, infer, and cite text evidence to support their answers. They will also need to be organized in their reading approach.

Appendix B

## Games to Enhance Analytical Thinking Skills

Many mass-market games can be used to hone analytical thinking skills. Some suggested games which target analytical thinking are listed here.

- ❏ **Set** is a card game which consists of 81 unique cards that vary in four features (shape, color, shading, number). There are three possibilities for each feature shape (diamond, squiggle, or oval), color (red, green, or purple), shading (solid, striped, or open), and number of shapes (one, two, or three). To make a set, the three cards must have features that are either all the same or all different. For example, three striped purple squiggles, two striped red diamonds, and one striped green oval would make a set because the shading is all the same type, the number of shapes is different, the shapes themselves are different, and the color is different. This game supports analytical thinking in that you must notice details, classify and organize the information, and think and think again to determine the *set*.
- ❏ **Outburst** is a game which is played with two teams. Teams take turns selecting a card on which a topic heading is printed, followed by a list of ten items that fall under the given topic. The object is to guess the ten items that were included on the card for the given topic. This game supports analytical thinking in that you must notice details, classify and organize your guesses under the correct topic, make an educated guess as to what would be on the card, and think and think again.
- ❏ **Scattergories** is a game for between two and six players in which the objective is to uniquely name objects within a category, given an initial letter, within a set time period. This game supports analytical thinking in that you must notice details, ask yourself questions, and make educated guesses as to what would be unique objects for the category.
- ❏ **Taboo** is a word-guessing partner game. The objective is for the player to give their partner clues to guess the word on the card without using the word itself or the five listed words on the card. This game supports analytical thinking in that you must notice details, ask yourself questions, think and think again, and make educated guesses as to what would be unique objects for the category.
- ❏ **Concept** is a guessing game in which the players must guess the concept. The player who has the concept provides hints by marking its attributes on the game board, while other players guess. This game supports analytical thinking in that you must notice details, ask yourself questions, think and think again, and make educated guesses as to what the category could be.

For Product Safety Concerns and Information please contact our EU representative GPSR@taylorandfrancis.com
Taylor & Francis Verlag GmbH, Kaufingerstraße 24, 80331 München, Germany